THE WINDS OF DESTINY

The Keepers of the Secret

By Willie Tee

Books by Willie Tee

The Winds of Destiny 1st Edition
The Winds of Destiny 2nd Edition
The Winds of Destiny-*The Keepers of the Secret*

The 1st & 2nd Editions of this book are the same, except that the 2nd Edition has reviews and was printed at a printing press. The 1st Edition of the book is printed on demand from a digital format. Both books are available for sale.

The Winds of Destiny – *The Keepers of the Secret*

Published by R&B Trading Company
P.O. Box 5171, Midlothian, VA 23112
Telephone: 804-739-8073
Email: Dwindsofdestiny@aol.com

ISBN: 0-9718784-4-7

Printed in the United States of America

The photograph on the cover of this book is used by permission from The Library of Congress, Washington, D.C. Prints and Photographs Division [reproduction number LC-8b29261u].

The Keepers of the Secret

Acknowledgements

I would like to acknowledge my late grandmother, who we affectionately called Granny and my mother in law, the late Mrs. Daisy. Both women inspired me. Mrs. Daisy, as I affectionately called her, was always a fair mother in law and never took sides during family disagreements. She encouraged her children, grandchildren, other relatives, and in laws to be decent Christians and pursue life goals in a meaningful way.

I thank my wife, Ruth, for being patient with my writing projects. She has more patience with me than I do myself.

Importantly, I would like to thank the many readers, some of which bought more than one copy of my book, The Winds of Destiny. An author needs an audience and readers of books are necessary for an author to succeed. I thank the many readers who have made my books a success.

Foremost, I must give humble thanks to the Heavenly Father, who guided my hand during the writing of this sequel.

I would be amiss if I did not mention my family, my mother, brother, sister, my children, aunts, uncles and cousins, who have supported my literary efforts. May God always bless you.

TABLE OF CONTENTS

FOREWORD

It is Thanksgiving evening, November 28, 2002 and I am sitting down at my personal computer to begin this sequel, *The Keepers of the Secret*, to my nonfiction book, "The Winds of Destiny". It is a cold fall night and the daytime temperature was about forty-five degrees Fahrenheit. It is now about eight thirty in the evening, and I sit sleepy eyed and full from the holiday feast. I decided on this holiday that I would write at least one page of the sequel to my controversial book.

This book is a historical account or memoir concerning my family's tragedies and triumphs. This book is not intended to demean the persons who are portrayed in it. It is designed to heal people who have encountered the same difficulties during their lives.

Writing novels, whether they are fictional or non-fictional is a time involved process and anyone that writes and publishes a novel should be given the appropriate recognition. I decided to write this sequel to further depict the saga of my family and our secret. The incredulous tragedy, which was kept as a secret from the youngest members or toddlers of my family, occurred during nineteen fifty-seven. In my opinion, it changed the destinies or lives of five generations of my family. This sequel is designed to depict our family life with its triumphs and tribulations after the tragedy of nineteen fifty-seven.

I feel that it is necessary for me to write about my family's past to obtain a greater appreciation for the lives that we lived, though there were good times and sad times. I am still suffering from some health problems that are relative to the tragedy, but I struggle to maintain a positive outlook towards life.

The biggest problem that mankind is facing, especially in the free world, is the "I want this now" syndrome. Unfortunately, some people will take great risks to get what they want. There seems to be little that rational people can do or say to warn some people of the risks of their behavior.

I think that all people need to realize that they own absolutely nothing. Tomorrow is not promised to anyone, because death is man's constant companion. We own nothing because we only exist here on earth for a limited period of time, therefore we only use what we acquire during life. Things that we acquire during our lives are left to our survivors after we are dead. People should acquire what they need to be reasonably comfortable.

I was working full time, going to college part time and doing a variety of home projects. This type of life style placed me in a stressful situation. I was encouraged to continue this type of lifestyle because of the supposed rewards at the end of the rainbow. In the end, the reward at the end of the rainbow was nearly a tombstone with my name engraved on it.

This sequel covers my family history from the year nineteen fifty-seven to present and it revisits some of the major incidents and scenes from the previous book, "The Winds of Destiny" to explain more in detail the aftermath of our family secret or tragedy. This book will depict rural life in the south during the twentieth century or the mid-nineteen hundreds. Of course, no historical depiction of any culture is complete without expounding on the people's beliefs and superstitions. People's beliefs are pivotal to any story, because certain beliefs motivate people to interact socially with other people from within and outside of their culture differently. If I neglected to tell you about the beliefs of the people in this sequel, in regards to the supernatural, it would be an incomplete story. I am obligated as a writer to depict circumstances and beliefs that are relative to the story I am telling. Then the story is both educational and entertaining.

Therefore, without further ado, I present to you this remarkable sequel of my family's saga. Will this sequel surpass "The Winds of Destiny", which people tout as one of the best books they had read. Well, I will let you readers be the judge of that. I hope that you enjoy reading my book and as always, I ask that you be flexible in your own feelings and beliefs about the supernatural.

----Willie Tee
Author

PROLOGUE

It has been several months now since the end of the U.S. military action in Afghanistan, which was prompted by the destruction of both towers of The World Trade Center by al-Qaida Terrorists on September 11, 2001. I started writing this book a year after this act of terrorism. In my opinion, the destruction of the towers is another sign of the times. It was foretold by biblical references and soothsayers or people with abilities to see into the future through either dreams or premonitions, that catastrophic incidents, world famine, and dissention worldwide would come before the end of days or the apocalypse. Though these signs of the times are significant, most people pay little attention to them. Man continues down a road of certain destruction.

I have been cautioned since the publishing of my previous book, "The Winds of Destiny", to refrain from divulging the contents of my dreams, which have been relative to some recent events. I know that prior to recent major events, some people had dreams or premonitions of them. I feel that for whatever reasons, warnings of these impending disasters were not heeded. Perhaps the world's destiny, which will involve an Apocalypse, is inescapable.

In Afghanistan, during the fall and winter of 2001, the Grim Reaper opened the gates of eternity to many al-Qaida terrorists and their Taliban allies. With President George W. Bush as our country's leader, a rapid and deadly military retaliation was certain and then swiftly orchestrated. Advanced U.S. military weaponry sent many terrorists and their allies into eternity. In my opinion, military battle is not an option for the enemy when given the awesome power of the U.S. military and its allies. Death and destruction are as certain as the rising and the setting of the sun.

Negotiations are really the only logical means of handling world issues, because some nations are now joining together as powerful coalitions to combat the evils of the world.

Though nations are forming coalitions, I can still envision the Four Horsemen of the Apocalypse. The horsemen sit battle ready upon their immortal steeds. The Four Horseman sit and wait patiently, as time is not relative to the task that might be soon at hand.

Tyranny, hate and evilness will not stand when the Horsemen ride. The dead will lie scorched and burnt upon the fields of battle. Who will mourn their stupidity?

I find it unconceivable that evildoers commit horrendous crimes with the notion that they will live spiritually afterwards at elevated levels. Needless to say, they condemn themselves to a certain hell, where they will suffer the burdens of their evil acts. In the end, they and all others with the same ideology will suffer destruction right here on earth.

It appears at this point, that Armageddon is right on schedule. Lies and deceit at the highest levels of governments worldwide continue. It is quoted in the Holy Scriptures that the meek shall inherit the earth. I believe this because the meek are sincere in their diplomacy with no outlook for gain. Therefore, the super powers of the world need to come to the negotiations table honestly with both hands outstretched and empty, and without treachery in their hearts.

I did not intend to belabor the problems of the world here at the beginning of my book. It is intended as encouragement for peace worldwide. So, with arms open wide, lets embrace each other and preserve our world for an eternity.

First, we must feed the hungry and care for the ailing, which is a crucial step towards disembodying ourselves of evil thoughts and actions. Then we must reduce violence in the streets and practice better gun control.

The Keepers of the Secret

CHAPTER ONE

In Search Of My Paternal Grandmother

I had met Brandy Davis, a young black lady in her early twenties, on April 6, 2002 at the Azalea Festival Arts & Craft Show, in the downtown sector of Wilmington. I had driven my truck, with plaques attached to both front doors, in the early morning parade of the Azalea Festival. I drove proudly through the streets and waved at cheering crowds of people. My cousins, Andrea and Evette and their children accompanied me. It was a dream come true, because as a child, I had often watched the parade as a spectator. Back then, I wished that I could have been in the parade myself.

After participating in the street parade, I set up a booth. I then sold and autographed my book, *The Winds of Destiny, 2nd Edition.* During the afternoon hours, I saw a young black lady with short cropped hair, but attractive in appearance, with a television cameraman. I noticed that the young lady was a television news reporter for WECT, Channel 6. WECT was the only television station broadcasting at Wilmington, North Carolina and the surrounding areas during the late 1950s, when I was growing up as a child. This particular television station was a reminder of my past life and invoked many memories of my past.

I approached Brandy and told her that I was an author. I asked if she would accept a copy of my book. Brandy, who impressed me as being very self-confident, eyed me in a speculative way and announced that she would accept the book. I asked the young lady her name and she responded, "I am Brandy Davis." I decided that the name suited her, because "Brandy" is an alcoholic drink that is dark and strong. The young news lady impressed me as being person of strong character and integrity. As someone, who was all about business, while on the job.

It was strange that I had left George, my brother, in charge of sales at the booth, while I wandered off in search for a restroom. Reflecting back on it, I would have not bumped into Brandy Davis, who had stopped about a block from my booth to do some filming, otherwise. Brandy would play a key role in the televising of my new book and my family's secret.

Brandy Davis had an inquisitive look on her face when she accepted the book from me. Brandy was at the Arts and Craft Show to produce a segment for a television show. I hoped that destiny or fate would land me a television interview after Brandy read my book. Without doubt, I was seizing the opportunity to garner some publicity for my book. I was impressed with the young lady. I felt that she would do an excellent job if she decided to do a news story about my book. I often tell readers during my book signings nowadays that they can shape their destinies by taking specific actions to change or improve things in their lives.

My book had already received rave reviews from readers. I rationalized that my book would stimulate the interest of this young but seasoned television reporter.

A week later, I received an email and telephone call from Brandy Davis. Brandy stated, "Willie, I want to interview you for a televised news segment. Can you come to Wilmington on April 26, 2002 to accomplish this?" I was ecstatic but paused to conceal my excitement. I then told Brandy that I would meet her that date to do an interview. Brandy also asked me to bring my brother along, who she had met when I gave her an autographed book. I told Brandy that my brother would be delighted to accompany us. I surmised that Brandy had found my brother as intriguing as myself. We are of similar height, build, and facial appearance. Anyone meeting us would quickly ascertain that we are brothers. I also told Brandy that I would locate the grave of my paternal grandmother prior to the interview by contacting my father's relatives at Pender County, North Carolina. I had never visited the gravesite, which was an issue discussed on the previous editions of my book.

In my book "The Winds of Destiny", I mentioned that my father was going to show me where his mother was buried during September or October of 1997, but my father died from injuries he sustained in a fight with a woman friend during that time period. I knew very few of my father's relatives because he rarely took us on visits to the small rural town of Pender County, North Carolina where his mother and him resided prior to her untimely and tragic death. However, my brother

George is very inquisitive, therefore I telephoned him and asked him to contact cousins of my father that still reside in that area.

A day later, I received a telephone call from George. He explained that he had contacted a younger first cousin of our father who knew where our paternal grandmother gravesite was located. My father's relative also contacted the present owner of the property where my paternal grandmother is buried. He agreed to show us her gravesite. I was very ecstatic over this development. However, I was also reluctant in some ways to see the final revelation of my family secret by a visit to the gravesite.

I counted the days. As the time approached for me to make this historical trip to North Carolina to find my paternal grandmother's grave, I pondered my good fortune. I had always envisioned myself finding my paternal grandmother's grave with television cameras documenting this historical event involving my family's history. It was amazing that I had decided to be a participant in the Azalea Festival at Wilmington by driving my truck in the street parade. I had a printing company at Richmond, Virginia create two signs, which depicted the front cover of my book, my name and the title of the book. I had attached the signs to both doors of my pickup truck.

Some people might say that I am lucky. However, I will quote a state championship middle school basketball coach who was my teacher at D.C. Virgo at Wilmington, North Carolina during the early nineteen seventies. The basketball team that he coached was integrated with both black and white players. Mr. William Dudley, a black man, coached his team to victory within a short time after the integration of public schools. Mr. Dudley would often say, "To be successful in this life, you got to be a go getter. Go and get what you want, because it will not come to you." This simple phrase has been a motivator for me all of my life, because Mr. Dudley was a role model for black youths during my younger years. He always stood his ground and did what was right.

On 26 April 2002, my brother George and I met Brandy Davis and a cameraman at a Hardee's Restaurant in the rural area of New Hanover County, North Carolina. It was about ten miles from Wilmington. I was driving my truck with George accompanying me. We escorted Brandy and her cameraman, who was driving a Channel Six WECT TV van, to Pender County, North Carolina or about thirty miles from where we had met. Pender County is a rural county and one of its cities is Burgaw, North Carolina, where I was born. I pointed out the many pigpens that were situated off of the rural highway. I chuckled at the hogs and pigs that were lazing in the sun with their bristle hide bodies covered in mud. Later, upon our arrival at my paternal mother's gravesite, Brandy Davis made remarks about the pigs and chuckled.

As we drove up the county highway I noticed a road sign that directed us to the small rural town where my father and my paternal grandmother once lived. We turned off the main highway onto a smaller two way paved road. Though it was late April, the temperature was sweltering and it was about one hundred degrees under the shade. The air conditioner in my truck blew at medium speed and kept my brother and I fairly cool despite the hot outdoors temperature. The road ahead of us snaked and curved as we drove. I noticed two small churches. A couple of small country stores and houses were spread sporadically along the sides of the country road.

I recalled that we had visited my father's house during 1963, which he inherited from his mother after her death, about thirty-eight years earlier. I remembered the house being tall, though it was a one story colonial. The house was situated high on a hill off the roadway.

We visited the house when I was about eight years old, and it was elegantly furnished. There were French doors leading into the dining room. The house had a high ceiling.

Years later, when I was about fourteen years old, I would travel through the area as a farm hand and notice that the house had deteriorated badly and was uninhabitable. I could never determine why my father did not sell the house, rent it, or live in it. I was told about the tragic killing of my paternal grandmother when I was thirteen years old. I was two years old during 1957, when Pa Daddy or my maternal grandfather killed her. As time progressed, my father did not pay taxes on the land. Later, the land and the dilapidated house were sold in an auction by the tax collector. My father made no efforts to pay the taxes or do anything in a positive way to save the house and land. It seemed that a huge windstorm came along and blew the house and land into oblivion, because it was no longer a part of our lives.

The means by which my paternal grandmother, Erdell, purchased the house was suspected. There were stories that my paternal grandmother immediately helped herself to the contents of a safe that belonged to a wealthy uncle upon his death. It reminds me of an old adage about ill-gotten possessions. The adage reminds us that such possessions are easily obtained and then easily lost. There is an irony attached to ill-gotten possessions.

Nowadays, I am older and wiser and can understand that the house was only a reminder of the good times that my father enjoyed there with his mother. He had loved his mother dearly and though he lived in the house for about four years after her death, the memories that the house possessed were too painful for him.

After four years of living alone, my father decided to leave the house, which had become a tomb of unbearable past memories. He reunited with my mother, a woman whom he loved dearly, and his three children. My father was forced to separate from my mother the awful night of the tragedy. My father was fully aware that his abuse and neglect of my mother had created a situation that caused his father in law to retaliate.

He would often ponder how he had foolishly failed to see the true character of his father in law. My father had heard some stories about the old man's strictness and the fear that his father in law generated within his family in the operation of the small family farm. My father would sometimes say during the years of my development from an adolescent to a youth that his father in law had the burden of providing for nine children. He implied that this could have been a factor that influenced his father in law's strict disposition and fierce behavior.

My father was human and deep within him, his anger smothered over the brutal killing of his mother. My father would carry this burden of anger and shame until the day that he died. Without doubt, my father would sometimes remember the night a shadowy phantom stood at the door of his car and in a booming and angry voice ordered him to get out of the car. Then he would see the face of the phantom clearly and realize that he had misjudged the person standing before him. He had misjudged his father in law or a man we called "Pa Daddy." Perhaps my father had been blinded by his preoccupation of money and the wealth that it brings. So blinded by stinginess and greed that he would not see the neglect and abuse that wreaked havoc on those that he loved. In the end, money would also cause his own demise. Often it is said that the love for money is the root of all evil. It is also the root of some people's doom. My father would sometimes awaken from his dreams with a start after the booming explosion of a gun.

I know that my father would often regret that he did not get out of his car that night to confront the anger of Pa Daddy. However, he was frozen with fear and apprehension to the car seat, like a small bird frozen to a tree limb in the dead of winter.

Nowadays, I sometime question whether it was fruitful for my father to reunite with my mother. There were many dark times in my father and mother's household, when my father's anger would explode over the killing of his mother by his father in law. Since his father in law was never available to feel the burnt of my father's anger, it was transferred to my mother, my siblings, and me. It was sometimes difficult living with my father, but the positive things that he taught us children overshadowed the turmoil.

However, prior to my father's death during nineteen nincty-seven, he would also be confronted by a person wielding a shotgun during nineteen seventy-four. My father met a man who was about his age and they became friends. The man's name was "Buster". Later, their friendship was strained by the appearance of a woman into the situation. Apparently, Buster was already acquainted with the woman and it appeared to Buster that my father was encroaching on the relationship that Buster enjoyed with this particular woman. Buster and my father had a verbal dispute over the matter and he confronted my father with a shotgun. Buster shot my father, and he fell to the ground with his left arm dangling and bleeding. It was rumored that if the ambulance had arrived one minute later than it did, that my father would have died from blood loss. My father was transported to a hospital at Wilmington, North Carolina by ambulance where a doctor removed his badly severed arm. He would retain only his right arm and would be a one armed man for the rest of his life.

The loss of my father's arm would only increase the bitterness in his heart, which resided there from his mother's death and over time, the bitterness would cause him to seek some sort of revenge. His revenge and the price he paid to obtain it will be outlined in the next sequel to this book.

My father was never able to forgive his father in law for the tragic events of that horrid night. He would never ever speak with his father in law again after that tragic night. Nor would my father, William, ever be seen in the company of his father in law again. His wound was of the kind that would never heal over time. This was my one of father's burdens from the tragedy. My father's other burden was the guilt that he carried for being instrumental in causing the death of his mother. If only my father had cared more for my mother's health than wealth, then his father in law would have had no reason to confront him with a shotgun.

It was ironic that my father's mother died from a shotgun blast during the year nineteen fifty-seven. Then my father almost died of a shotgun blast during the year nineteen seventy-four or seventeen years later.

It was strange that though his father in law

was after my father with a shotgun, he escaped without injury that night during nineteen fifty-seven. However, my father's mother was killed. One would have to admit that this is a chilling revelation when you consider that both a mother and son were shot with shotguns. Stranger yet, is the fact that my father lived forty years after his mother's death, but they both died in years that ended with the number seven. *1957* and *1997* were the years of my paternal grandmother's death and my father's death respectively. They both were killed and did not die naturally.

There were **seven** people in my father's car the night of the incident during *1957.* It is obvious that *seven* is a relative number in this strange equation. I will elaborate further and note that both of my maternal grandparents died on the date *27 February* but not the same year. However, they died *seven years* apart. Pa Daddy died **27 February** *1994* and Granny died **27 February 2001**. A lady who owned a tombstone business stated that she had never prepared headstones for a wife and husband who had died the same month and day, unless they died together in an accident.

We know of the significance of **666** or the sign of the devil. The number **777** also has significance. According to some writings, 777 is normally a good number, but evil forces can manipulate this number.

I am not finished yet with the oddness of certain situations, because prior to my father losing his arm during **1974**, I was stationed at West

Germany. This was **17** years after my paternal grandmother's death or killing.

I had a reoccurring dream on at least four occasions before my father's arm was shot off. I dreamed that I was in a dimly lit funeral home or chapel. Several feet in front of me is a black coffin with half of the lid raised. I had a desire to approach the coffin to look in. I am apprehensive about looking in because I felt that someone of significance was in the coffin. I awakened and was unable to look inside of the coffin.

The same dream occurs a second and third time and the dreams were about three to four days apart. I failed during the second and third dreams to look inside the coffin and awakened quickly each time. Finally, during the fourth dream, I walk slowly towards the coffin and peek in. I see my father inside of the coffin. He is dressed splendidly in a dark suit.

I have often heard that dreams are signs of things that will occur during the future. However, this dream seemed to carry an obvious message. About four weeks after the fourth dream, I was informed by my platoon sergeant that my father had been shot. I telephoned my mother and she further disclosed that my father had lost his arm during a shooting incident and almost bled to death. I was devastated and felt a twinge of guilt, because I did not telephone my father from Germany and warn him about the dream.

Therefore, my father lost his arm in a shooting incident 17 years after his mother was gunned down. The number 7 appears again within a number.

However, as I grew older over the years and experienced other dreams or premonitions, I learned that I could really change nothing. It seemed that one way or the other the dreams would be fulfilled despite any interference on my part. I then acquired a sleeping disorder or apnea during the nineteen eighties, and I dream only rarely now. It seems that the sleeping disorder is punishment for either my interference or interest in my dreams. In my opinion, a person can really make a mess of things by interceding into situations that will occur in the future according to dreams. Nowadays, I let dreams occur and note that the dreams were accurate predictions.

My thoughts about the past were interrupted, when I saw the address numbers on a rural mailbox, which was our destination. I was apprehensive about visiting my paternal grandmother's gravesite, because this visit would end my lifelong quest to visit the gravesite. A visit to the gravesite was the event that I needed for closure concerning my family's dark secret. I pulled into the driveway of the residence or doublewide modular home and parked. Brandy Davis and her cameraman parked their van beside my truck, and we disembarked from our vehicles.

A medium built black man who wore a cap met us at the grounds of the residence. The man identified himself as Johnny. I thanked him for assisting us with our search. Johnny stated that after he purchased the plot of land, he was told to be mindful while clearing the land of brush and trees because three graves were located there. Johnny stated that my relatives told him to be careful of where Miss Ert or my paternal grandmother was buried. The heat that day for late April was extreme. It was at least one hundred degrees Fahrenheit or hotter.

We then walked a short distance from Johnny's residence and located three graves in a wooded area. I noted that one gravestone had the full name of the deceased on it and the surname was that of my father's aunts, uncles and cousins on his mother's side of the family. I then saw two small stones among the shrubbery and vines on the ground. George and I crouched close to the ground and examined the weathered stones tentatively. We noted that the stones bore initials of the deceased and determined that the stone or grave marker with initials "ET" with a space between the letters was the gravesite of my paternal grandmother Erdell, who was also nicknamed "Ert". The "R" between the letters "E" and "T" had weathered away.

The WECT cameraman was filming the area while my brother and I continued out examination of the gravesite. Brandy Davis stood on the edge of the wooded area in a clearing, because the area we explored was laden with briars and thorny vines. By pushing the thorny vines away from us gingerly with our fingers, George and I were able to move around the gravesite without hindrance.

Our exploration of the wooded area brought

back fond memories of years past when George and I were adolescents and we use to explore the woods near my grandparents home. Though we are now adults and older than the days of our youth, our relationship as brothers has never changed. There was always a very close kinship between us and we never had any major disagreements. I wished that this were the situation between my sister, Helen, and I. Helen is the oldest child and I am the middle child, and there were sometimes conflicts between us. I always felt that my sister, Helen, had a domineering personality, which I would always meet with a gruff resistance. I always felt that she was overly critical of others, but then I discovered that I am overly critical myself at times. This gives weight to the argument that people with similar personalities are often in disagreement.

After foraging the area and filming the gravesite, we thanked Johnny for his assistance. I had a variety of mixed emotions that day about us locating my paternal grandmother's grave. Johnny asked me if I planned on moving my paternal grandmother's remains from his property. He stated that he would have no objections. I looked at Johnny and our eyes locked. I told him that it was my sincere intention to have her remains moved and that it would be in keeping with a promise that I made to my father.

Brandy Davis had looked intently at me while I conversed with Johnny. My facial expressions were very solemn, because despite the success of finding my paternal grandmother's grave, my heart was heavy with emotions. However, I did not blame my maternal grandfather or my father for my paternal grandmother's death. My father told me several months prior to his death in nineteen ninety-seven that he desired to be buried beside his mother. Of course, time and other factors had prevented him from being buried beside her and my father was buried in an immaculate cemetery near where I spent most of my adolescent years at Wilmington.

My goal is to transfer his mother remains to a grave near my father's. Then and only then, will this saga of my life be complete. I will have full closure then. But then, I have always been a man of my word. Once I make a promise to accomplish a task, grim as it may be, I will do it. I also relish seeing the astonished faces of critics who spend a lifetime berating others, when I fulfill certain promises. I see nothing wrong in correcting certain wrongs of the past, even if I have to spend my personal money to accomplish it. I am very sentimental about deceased family members who were not given the appropriate honors and respect at the time of their deaths.

I had noticed during our trip to my paternal grandmother's grave that the house that my father had inherited from his mother after her death had vanished from sight. During earlier years, the nineteen sixties, the house sat up on a hill near the rural paved highway that trekked through the small North Carolina village. The area where the house once stood is now covered with trees and brush. There is nothing visible to indicate that a house every stood at that location. Perhaps one day, when

I am more prosperous, I might endeavor to build a replica of the house that once stood there. I have always felt that life is about a family's past and future. I would live for periods of time at the replica home in remembrance of my family's past life. I did live in the house as an infant for two years prior to the tragic killing of my paternal grandmother at my maternal grandparent's farm during 1957.

On our return trip, my brother, Brandy Davis, her cameraman, and I stopped on a dusty dirt packed road near the wooded area where the house once stood. I attempted to enter the woods to survey the site for remains of the house, but the woods were too dense. I parted some brush with my hands and peered in to the thick foliage, but could see only four inches ahead of me.

I returned to my truck and told Brandy Davis that I could not see any remains of the house. We then drove back to my deceased maternal grandparent's property at New Hanover County. Brandy and her cameraman then did some filming of the old farm to include Granny's old house. George and I talked on camera about our family's dark secret and the burdens that we carried. I concluded my narration by stressing the importance of families being in unity with each other. I pointed out that unified families have fewer tragedies.

The television crew completed filming my maternal grandparent's house and later created a news segment that aired on Channel Six, WECT during May 2002.

Aunt Linda reminded me after Granny's

death, that we needed to make haste in settling her burial affairs and other issues, because Granny never liked unpaid debts and obligations. I have that same mentality nowadays myself. I believe that no one should get himself or herself so indebted that they cannot repay their obligations. I also believe that we the living should handle the burial and estates of the deceased with honesty and integrity. The deceased should be buried in keeping with the burial insurance policies they possessed and the value of their estates.

I have seen a few graves without tombstones in our family plot, though the deceased left a sufficient estate to cover the cost of a tombstone. Regardless of the sum of money that the deceased left behind, the surviving relatives should pay for such arrangements. If family members practice this, then everyone could be assured that they will get a tombstone when they die. I feel that it is a betrayal to grab the deceased's estate and bury the person in a pine box with no grave marker. If I were ever that inconsiderate, I hope someone would beat me to my senses.

Some people are naïve and foolish. They do horrible things after their relatives die and think that no one else in the family harbors hard feelings against them. On any given day, I can walk through cemeteries where my relatives are buried and can remember several good deeds that they did for others and me during their lifetime. I will never forget their good deeds. I will also never forget the people who betrayed them after these relatives were dead and gone. It makes the blood boil in one's veins to think of some people's treachery during the past. Well, I will leave this alone for now, but one day I am going to remind some people about what they did not do. I think that during our golden years, when we are hobbling around on walking canes, I will remind certain people of their treachery. Hoping that we will be too old to fight physically over my comments

I must not forget that this day was of importance, because I located my paternal grandmother's gravesite. This was another vital step in the fulfillment of my own destiny. I believe that I survived the clutches of death several times to fulfill my destiny. I am suspicious about what my final destiny might be. I am living on borrowed time because of advanced aging from my military service. However, death is not my greatest concern. At this point, I am moving to correct some wrongs and problems that were created by my ancestors during the past. I hope that my actions will prevent some of my relatives from repeating events that occurred in our family's past.

In my book, *The Winds of Destiny*, I described how stinginess, greediness, meanness and arrogance caused a terrible tragedy in my family. These elements are still present within my family and like a crouching tiger can spring forth at anytime with deadly consequences. People often talk about lessons learned from the past. We do well to heed these lessons.

I find it strange that some people cannot fully

comprehend that they will die one day. It is a simple equation of subtraction and addition. Subtract your close relatives who have died and add those who are newly born. It means that we who are living now will die and will be subtracted, while infants will be born into our families as additions. No one is exempted from the equation, and we all will depart this life at some point in time.

The tragedy was kept as a secret from me until I was thirteen years old. Really, this secret kept me from paying homage to my paternal grandmother, who lied in a pitiful grave in the woods. I wonder how many people stumbled upon her grave in the woods and asked, "Who is buried here? What kind of life did this person have before death came?"

The dead cannot speak from the grave, but a wandering person would assume that other people loved the deceased. The deceased smiled, laughed and cried during life. Since I am realistic, when I visit gravesites, I conclude that graves are relative to my own destiny one day. Death does not discriminate, regardless of how handsome or beautiful or how wealthy or poor a person might be. It will visit us all someday.

The person in the grave or my paternal grandmother held me in her arms when I was an infant. She cooed me to sleep. She changed my diapers and bathed me. My paternal grandmother fed and clothed me. This I know, because this is what all grandmothers do.

Now the time draws near for me to bring her

from a dismal grave and lay her beside her only child or my father. When my task is done, I will lay beautiful flowers upon her new grave and erect a tombstone at the head of her grave. I shall inscribe on it, "Here rests a grandmother, who is a secret no more." I will bow my head and remember that I originated through her. I understand even better now that death is inevitable after we are born.

One day, I will lie in a grave, perhaps near my paternal grandmother, and fulfill my destiny of life and death. But, now it is time for me to journey back into the past again, to my family's farm on the outskirts of Wilmington, North Carolina. It was during a time of racial strife and an evolving modern world. The nineteen fifties through nineteen seventies were the good old times, a time of youth and better health for some of us older folks. However, it was not always the best of times, as you readers will learn.

CHAPTER TWO

A Day to Remember

I drove my truck slowly up the paved U.S. Highway that I had walked many times as a adolescent during the late nineteen fifties and early nineteen sixties. This is the month of February 2002. It has been over a year now since Granny's death. I have visited her grave on several occasions to pay my respects. However, I have not been inside of Granny's old house since her death. I avoid going inside of her house because it would only confirm that Granny is no longer in the world of the living. Since Granny was always at her house during my unannounced visits during the past, it is now hard for me to fathom or grasp that she is gone in a physical sense. Therefore, I am not living in a world of reality concerning her death. I will not enter her house, as it would destroy the barrier of disbelief that I have erected. Of course, some people might say that this is unhealthy. I wonder if I gave myself enough time to appropriately grieve Granny's death. I am not ashamed to admit that I cried after leaving the hospital that gray winter day during the early hours of the morning.

Aunt Linda had telephoned me at Motel Super Eight on Market Street, during the early morning hours of February 27, 2001. In fact she telephoned me right after Cousin Andrea, who was tending to Granny at the hospital, had called.

Cousin Andrea had been the bearer of bad news. She told me, in a tearful voice, that Granny had passed. I thanked Cousin Andrea for the notification and after some tossing and turning, I fell into a fitful sleep. An hour later, I was awakened by the shrill ringing of the telephone in my motel room and upon answered the phone. Aunt Linda commanded me to come by the hospital. I asked Aunt Linda, whose voice was filled with sorrow, if I would be allowed to view Granny's remains. She informed me that I could view Granny. After our short but sorrowful conversation, I pulled my weary body out of bed and took a quick shower. I dressed quickly and drove hurriedly to Cape Fear Valley Hospital.

I drove from the motel towards the hospital and many thoughts swirled through my mind. I did not want to accept the fact that Granny was dead, though she was one hundred and one years old at the time of her death. In my opinion her death was unacceptable, despite her age or longevity. When people live as long as Granny, I consider them practically immortal, therefore their deaths are unconceivable.

Well, I was in no hurry to arrive at the hospital, because viewing Granny's remains would only confirm that she was no longer in the world of the living.

After driving in circles for ten additional minutes and making wrong turns, I arrived at Cape Fear Valley Hospital. I summoned an elevator and traveled to the floor and room where Granny resided. I saw several of my relatives, Aunt Della and her husband Preston, Aunt Linda and her husband, Stephanie, my sister Helen, and Cousin William standing in the hallway with live plants in their hands. I thought that it was remarkable or strange that they had already brought flowers to the hospital after hearing of Granny's death. I determined later during a conversation with them that they had removed flowers and live plants from Granny's room after she expired. It was odd that I never noticed so many flowers and plants in Granny's room during my visits there.

  With my head bowed low and a heart filled with grief, I walked down the long gray corridors of the hospital towards the room where Granny's remains lied. I am of the Christian belief. In my opinion, Granny's death was a new beginning.

Surely our hearts are filled with grief,
But still we believe,
That one day we will see you again,
At another place and time.

Come let us gather and mourn,
With our tearful faces pointed upwards,
Our wails and cries reverberating
Throughout these hallow halls.

We will always remember your love,
Your unending generosity,
Your sharing and caring,
Until, we see you again.

Chapter Three

Growing up on the Farm

"Willieeeee Teeeee", Granny exclaimed in a loud gruff voice. "Get on up and come to breakfast." I was only partially asleep that cold winter morning during the winter of 1960. I smelled the odors of frying bacon and home made baked biscuits during the early hours of the morning as Granny prepared breakfast on her old propane gas stove. Small puffs of condensation rolled from my mouth, as I moved from under the warm quilts that covered our bed. Quilts were piled on top of beds during the harsh North Carolina winters. The quilts, combined with the body heat of other bed companions, kept us fairly warm at night.

My feet shriveled when they struck the cold wood floor of the bedroom. I got out of bed and dressed hurriedly and awakened George, my younger brother, who was almost three years old. I was older than him and almost five years old. George and I pulled on one-piece zip up padded jump suits with the boots attached. We then grinned broadly at each other and marched towards Granny's kitchen. We paused for a few seconds near the cast iron potbelly wood stove, which was the main source of heat for the den and kitchen area. The bedrooms were closed off as well as the living room and these rooms were unheated. Aunt Virginia, who was perhaps fifteen years old, Uncle

Leon who was fourteen years old, and Aunt Linda, who was perhaps ten years old had already departed for school on the county school bus that stopped on weekdays on the shoulder of the paved two lane major highway. The highway was located a short distance from my grandparents three bedroom single level house. Aunt Virginia, Aunt Linda and Uncle Leon were the teenage sisters and brother of my mother, Annie. A rutted dirt road, almost a city block in length, extends from the paved main highway to the farmhouse.

George and I waddled across the vinyl floor of the kitchen and approached Granny, who was dressed in a gingham style dress that was hemmed well below her knee. Granny wore a flowery apron around her waist. Granny was a short and stout dark brown coffee color skinned woman, who was slightly rotund, but solid as an oak tree. There was no fat or flab on Granny's physique. Granny lived on a tobacco farm from 1900, when she was born, to the present time of 1960. She was one of seven children in her family. Granny had two sisters and two brothers living during 1960. Two of her older brothers had passed on into eternity some years earlier as well as both of Granny's parents. Needless to say, rigorous farm work had transformed Granny and her siblings into sturdy and powerful farmhands. This was also the case with Granny's seven daughters and two sons and her numerous grandchildren. We were human powerhouses. With broad smiles on our faces, George and I strode into the kitchen area and sat on chairs at a large wooden table. With a broad smile creasing her face, Granny heaped grits, fried eggs and ham onto two large plates. She then gingerly grabbed two homemade biscuits from a pan and placed them, one at a time, onto the two plates of food. As I devoured my food, I glanced out of the window of my grandparent's one story, three-bedroom house, which was constructed of a wood frame and sturdy wooden siding.

Over the years, or later on, the siding of the old house would be painted white, green, blue and other colors.

I peered out of the window of the house that cold wintry morning of February 1960 and spied the small field at the side of the house. The field contained some wilted vegetables, which were the remnants of the fall harvest. Small gray and black sparrows hippity hopped across the barren field and would pause to peck at wilted plants and grass with their beaks. I often wondered how such frail looking birds could survive the harsh southern winters. I would learn later when I became older that birds have layers of feathers, which protect them from the frigid winter temperatures. As a five-year-old and an adolescent, I was curious about every creature that I saw. I had a keen interest in birds or fowls because they could fly and glide effortlessly through the air, while I remained earthbound.

I looked beyond the field and noticed that about one city block from Granny's house and in a clearing was a large shanty with an outhouse situated at its rear. The shanty belonged to my Aunt

Peggy and her son Howard, who was nicknamed "Snap" and about nine years old during this time period. This was an appropriate nick name for my Cousin Howard because his temper could flare easily if someone disagreed with a point that he was making during a conversation. However, if a person diplomatically explained to Snap that he was mistaken, he would flash a broad grin and thank the person profusely for correcting him. But if someone made unkind remarks to Snap about making a mistake, his eyes would flash and he would loudly defend his remarks. If someone wanted to evolve the situation to a physical confrontation, then, Snap was willing and able.

It seemed that Snap and my Uncle John despite their age differences of about fifteen years would often have heated discussions to defend their positions during their arguments. Though they both were often courteous of each other, Uncle John with his light coffee colored complexion and Snap with his dark brown complexion seem to have more confrontations between themselves than the other family members at a whole. Despite their shades of coloring, both Snap and Uncle John were handsome in appearance. I made observations during my adolescence that my family as a whole consisted of relatives who were Mulatto colored to dark brown in complexion. My grandfather, Pa Daddy was a Mulatto with Black and Native American features. My Granny was dark brown with black and Native American facial features. My grandparent's children ranged from dark brown to Mulatto in appearance but we all had handsome facial features despite the color variances. It never failed that Uncle John would make a comment about Snap's darker features during their arguments. This was the same as throwing a gallon of gasoline inside of the wood burning potbelly stove. During incidents of this nature, Granny would fiercely intervene and vigorously chastise the parties involved. Granny would often comment that she had never seen such bad behavior between two people during her lifetime. She would encourage Uncle John and Snap to pray and seek God for guidance.

There was seldom a dull moment around my grandparent's farm. Sometimes, after an argument was defused, some other relatives would comically recall other relative's antics during the argument. Then there would be peals of laughter emitting from my relatives who were audience to the fiasco. My Uncle Leon, who was about fourteen years old during 1960, was most avid at comically portraying people involved in arguments after they occurred. We adolescents of the family would roll across the yard laughing or fall off chairs. Even the parties involved in the argument, would then realize the ridiculousness of the situation they created and laugh also. Hell, we never hurt each other during the worst of disagreements and grudges were not held very long. I feel, even today, that the love that a family has for each other as individuals should always overshadow petty disagreements and grievances.

I then redirected my attention to the delicious meal of grits, homemade biscuits, thick fried bacon, and eggs that decorated the plate before me. I began to devour the tasty meal with a broad smile on my face. Granny's face beamed as George and I greedily devoured our meals. It always seemed that Granny was very pleased to see her children and grandchildren eat her delicious meals with wild abandon. Without doubt, my Granny was a skilled cook, who could feed from two people to fifty people with quick precision. Granny's moves in and around her kitchen seemed choreographed and she moved effortlessly while preparing meals. The heavy black cast iron skillets and pots were like feathers in her strong sturdy hands.

After our meal was completed, George and I glided effortlessly off the high bar stools at the kitchen bar. George, who was about three years old, became interested in an early morning cartoon on the television and soon he was laughing at the antics of the cartoon characters on the television. We had one television channel back during the 1960s and it was WECT Channel Six, which broadcasts out of Wilmington, North Carolina, a prosperous seaport city. I put on a pair of mittens and flipped the hood of my padded one-piece body suit over my head. I pulled the drawstrings of the hood tight and tied them under my chin in a loose knot. I resembled an over stuffed rotund teddy bear. Granny chuckled when she saw how I was dressed. I looked upwards at Granny and she beamed a smile at me. Granny then quipped, "Where are you going bright eyes?"

This was an adoring phrase, "bright eyes" that old Granny, who was sixty years old, used when addressing me. I smiled and remarked, "Granny, I am going to get eggs from the hens." Granny nodded her approval, and I bounded out the rear door of her house.

I then made a beeline for the chicken house, which was a medium sized wooden shack made of surplus unpainted lumber. The roof of the hen house was slanted, with the front of the roof pitched upwards and the rear of the roof slanted downwards. The roof was constructed with large sheets of silver colored galvanized tin. The elevation of the roof caused rain water to flow away from the entrance of shack when it rained.

Upon entering the hen house, I noticed that the hens were sitting inside of individual boxes that were on rickety platforms about three feet above the earthen floor of the shack. The boxes were partially filled with soft straw, which the hens rested on with their legs tucked under them. We called the chicken shack the "chicken coop". The hens began to cackle upon my approach. I reach deftly to the side of the first hen that was sitting on its egg. The hen pecked annoyingly at my hand with her sharp beak, as I reached under her and retrieved a large egg. I then visited where the other hens were roosting and deprived them of their eggs. I placed each egg carefully in a basket woven of straw and rushed out of the chicken coop back into the frigid morning air. The cold air stung my face and ears and my hands felt numb from the bitter cold.

Though winters were so cold and dreary at the farm, I always relished this time of year. The winter tested our sturdiness as a people. During the fall, we prepared for winter by slaughtering a fattened hog or two. We salted, hickory smoked, and froze the meat for the upcoming Thanksgiving and Christmas holidays, and for the hard cold winter season ahead.

We prepared "sweet potato beds" during the late fall by digging a wide and deep hole behind Granny's house and layering the bottom of the hole with pine needles from pine trees. On top of the layer of pine needles, we would place a layer of sweet potatoes that we harvested from my grandparent fields during the fall. My Aunt Linda, Uncle Leon, Cousin Howard, other cousins and myself would construct the sweet potato bed by alternating layers of sweet potatoes and pine needle until the bed was completed.

The objective was to bury the highest level of the layers of potatoes below the frost line. Well, the frost line is a depth down in the ground where the cold never freezes soil or whatever you care to bury there. It was important to place the uppermost layer of sweet potatoes below the frost line to keep them from becoming frostbitten or damaged by the cold. Sweet potatoes damaged by the cold are obvious because portions of the potatoes are hardened and look badly discolored. You will encounter a horribly bitter taste in your mouth if you eat a portion of a frost damaged potato. Sometimes if only a small portion of the potato is damaged, you can cut off the damaged portion and cook the rest. However it would still not be the best tasting sweet potato.

The thing about sweet potatoes is the numerous dishes you can make with them. With sweet potatoes, we made pies, sweet potato pudding, a casserole with an assortment of nuts, sweet potatoes with cracklings or pork rinds, candied yams, or just a sweet potato thrown on a plate either peeled or not peeled as a side item. Of course for the ultimate southern cuisine, there was sweet potato with possum. Well, I never have eaten possum, but some of my kin told me that it is a very greasy piece of meat. But sweet potatoes can sup up the grease from anything. I have no intentions of ever eating possum because that is one ugly creature, which looks like a big rat, and seems to grin at everyone that it meets.

I recall back during the early nineteen seventies of riding either with Uncle Jimmy P. or Uncle Jessie, who married my Aunts Virginia and Eloise respectively. Both men were well known throughout our family. Uncle Jimmy P. was a giant of a man with a very friendly disposition, but had the strength of an ox. Uncle Jessie was notorious for his fighting skills. It seems that he won many fights that most people would have lost by biting chunks of flesh out of his opponents' legs. I believe that Uncle Jessie also bit people in other places, but I will spare readers with faint hearts of the graphic details.

Well, while I was riding in a car with one of the aforementioned uncles, we spied a possum crossing a lonely paved country road. My uncle sped up and struck the possum by angling the trajectory of the car. He then exited the car rapidly and grabbed the possum, which was stunned but not injured and threw it in his car trunk. I was shocked because I never saw anyone hunt game with a car and retrieve it alive.

Upon our return to Granny's house, my uncle placed the possum in a cage and fed it vegetables to clean its digestive system out. I was further shocked to hear that the possum was scheduled for an evening meal as the main course. Well, the possum never made it to the menu because a visitor with a taste for possum paid my uncle a handsome price for it. I could not imagine that anyone would want to eat something so ugly that looked like a skunk, rat, cat, and who knows what else slapped together.

A few years later, during the late nineteen seventies, Uncle Jimmy P. would be shot and killed by an assailant. The man that I knew, as a gentle giant would be transported back to his home state of Georgia, from whence he came, and buried there. However, I will never forget Uncle Jimmy P., a giant of a man with a gentle heart.

We carry our fallen brother upon our
Broad and strong shoulders,
Back to his native soil,
With our faces saddened and wet with tears,
But he is in God's loving arms once more.

Come let us lay his coffin low,
Into the earths comfort once more.
Let us play sweet melodies on a horn,
And remember the day he was born.

He was born to die one day,
But is today better than any other?
When you lose a brother,
Who was like no other.

This evening we will drink and eat,
And remember grand things,
About our fallen brother,
Who we loved like no other.

The dark one stands there in the shadows,
Waiting there for you and me.
But tonight we celebrate the life
Of our fond brother,
Just like we did for the others.

Chapter Four

The County School Bus

When I was four years of age, Aunt Virginia taught we how to read some words. The first word that I learned to read was "war". I saw the word in a newspaper or magazine and asked Aunt Virginia what it meant. She told me that it involved soldiers from different countries fighting in combat and similar to the World War II movies that I watched as a child, though the Korean War Era had just barely ended.

My mother had been in the hospital for months and I only had vague memories of her. I had flash bulb memories of her walking thin and frail through my grandparent's house on wobbly legs. Since my mother was not available to care for my sister Helen, who was two years older than I, and my brother George, who was two years younger, Aunt Virginia and Granny took care of us. Aunt Virginia, a teenager, was slightly older than Aunt Linda and Uncle Leon, who were perhaps about ten years old during 1960.

Aunt Linda is the youngest child of my Granny's nine children and she was perhaps seven years old when the tragedy of nineteen fifty-seven occurred. However, Aunt Linda knew the circumstances of the tragedy and the identities of all parties that were involved, but she was sworn to secrecy like the adults. Cousin Howard was perhaps about six years old when the tragedy occurred. He was perhaps the only cousin of ours who also had knowledge of the secret or tragedy. It was amazing that children as adolescent as Aunt Linda and Cousin Howard kept the secret as well as the adults of our family. They would never tell us younger relatives. The adults would inform us when we became teenagers.

I know from growing up during the nineteen fifties and nineteen sixties that children were held to a higher level of accountability than children are nowadays. We children back then were also given incentive to be more accountable and it was called corporal punishment. It was an unpleasant way of punishing children for disobedience and bad behavior. The punishment, when applied to the buttocks with paddles, belts, switches or twigs from plants, caused pain and was something that we children preferred not to receive. Therefore, corporal punishment encouraged us to be on our best behavior most of the time.

As I recount the events of my life as a adolescent, years like 1959 seem so long ago when compared to now or the year 2004. Time has moved along so swiftly but not kindly in some respects. This is obvious when I look at my protruding belly.

During 1960, when I was almost five years old, I would see the yellow county school bus pull to a stop off the main paved highway in front of Granny's house. Despite the cold or heat of the winter and late spring seasons, I would run swiftly with my legs and arms pumping wildly towards the bus stop. I could hear the wind whistling through my clothes and hair as I ran. Needless to say, I was a very fast runner. As I ran, I would see Aunt Virginia, Aunt Linda and Uncle Leon get off the school bus with their books tucked under their arms and walk up the wide dirt packed road towards my grandparents house. It happened that one day during 1960, Aunt Linda and her siblings got off the bus and I ran to greet them. My sister, Helen, who was two years older than me got off the bus also.

Aunt Linda, who was about ten years old, with a lighter complexion than most of my relatives, broke into a wide grin and then laughed. I came to stop near her and then smiled broadly at her also. I knew from past encounters with Aunt Linda, that her broad smile and laugh always preceded a comment of interest that she would make. I then waited in anticipation for her to make a comment. Giggling, Aunt Linda stated, " Hi their Willie T. I am going to call you this name from now on, because I read about a boy with this name in a book at school today." So this is how I was given the name "Willie T", which is my nickname and not my Christian name. Many years later, during the year 2000, I would modify that nickname to "Willie Tee" and use it as my author's name for the original edition of this book.

Later, when I entered the first grade at elementary school my nickname once got me in a tricky situation with my teacher, Mrs. Devaughn. On the very first day of elementary school at Peabody Elementary School at Wilmington, North

Carolina, my father dropped me off to school. I noticed that my father knew Mrs. Devaughn, because she was his cousin. The year was 1961 and I was six years old. My relatives and parents called me "Willie T" and never my Christian name. The teacher called the attendance roll. When she announced my Christian name I did not respond, because I did not know my Christian name. Mrs. Devaughn became gruff, pointed at me, and told me to answer the roll when my name was called. I remarked, "Well, my name is Willie T." The teacher became upset and told me that the name she had just announced was my name. Mrs. Devaughn stated that I would respond in class when that name or my name was announced or called.

When I arrived at home after school, I approached my mother and told her about the incident at school. My mother Annie confirmed that the teacher was correct concerning my Christian name. I was shocked that no one ever told me my Christian name. Of course, the students in my class giggled when the teacher had corrected me concerning my name. Nowadays, I often laugh myself when I reminisce about when I caused confusion in school concerning my name. Of course, I was fortunate that first day of school that the confusion did not earn me a buttocks warming from Mrs. Devaughn's paddle. I still believe that my teacher was a master at delivering out corporal punishment, because I met few teachers later that could administer punishment the way that she did.

On occasions, I would see Granny with a brown package that contained two women pocketbooks or handbags. The handbags were made of new leather, and the smell of the new leather was intoxicating to my nostrils. Granny would remove the paper on the handbags and beam proudly at them. The handbags were a present from her husband or Pa Daddy. I was able to surmise that Pa Daddy or my maternal grandfather, who was away at the time, made the handbags. Because of my adolescence, I was not really interested in Pa Daddy's whereabouts and never asked anyone where he was. Of course, it was a secret where Pa Daddy was. Pa Daddy was serving a prison sentence of three to five years (fifteen year sentence) for the killing of my paternal grandmother or his son in law's mother. He would be released early for being a model prisoner.

In my world as an adolescent, guests and other people often appeared for short visits and then departed. I would surmise that they lived in houses up the road. My world was within the confines of my grandparent's farm. I had no interest in things that I could not see at a distance or comprehend.

I would discover many years later during my psychology and sociology classes in college that children five years of age like myself do not analyze situations in depth and make only casual observations of situations that occur around them.

As I matured, I would analyze situations more in depth and ask questions to come to a complete understanding of what I was seeing and hearing.

Later in life, I would analyze my observations, other's conversations and come to correct conclusions about existing situations. However, during my early adolescence, I was a babe in the woods as the adage goes and my knowledge was very limited.

I did not worry that my mother was not available, because I had Granny and my uncles and aunts carrying for me. On some warm spring days before school was out for the summer session, Uncle John would take my brother George and I in his black Studebaker to a nearby farm where he was employed for short periods of time during the planting season. Uncle John would park his car under a shade tree and instruct me to stay in the car with my younger brother while he worked.

It would be shady and cool under the large oak tree. Cool breezes of air, bountiful and rich with the fragrances of nature's flowers, would float in and out of the opened windows of the car. I was very obedient during my youth and did as my uncle instructed me. I had also sensed that my brother and I were the responsibility of my younger aunts and uncles, some of who were not adults yet and adult relatives. Therefore, I followed their instructions and made their supervision of me simple. Uncle John would plow a field with a tractor or a mule with plow. On the lunch hour, he would appear back at the car and open up a can of sweet potatoes or peaches. On occasions he would have sandwiches. We would share Uncle John's lunch and then he would return to his farming tasks.

At the end of the day, Uncle John would appear again for our trip back to Granny's farm. I would awaken from sleeping and dreaming of pleasant things. We would then drive back to my grandparent's farm. Granny, who had worked a whole day at some other farm or house as a maid, would be cooking up the evening meal. Granny would smile broadly when we entered the house near her kitchen. She would often exclaim, "My, my, you are finished for today. I am almost finished cooking. I am so happy to see you all." As always, tantalizing odors of cooking food would be wafting through the air.

Soon the county school bus would be bringing my uncle and aunts home from school. With a cloud of dust trailing behind me, I would run fast as I could up the dirt road to meet them. Meeting the school bus was a daily routine for me. Well, back during the nineteen sixties, I had some idle time on my hands and made my self feel important by running to the bus. I loved my uncle and aunts and taking time to run and meet them was a big event of the day for me. I will never forget the yellow county school bus.

Chapter Five

A Storm to Remember

A September morning during the late summer of the year nineteen sixty began in a strange and different way. I noticed that the sky was dark and foreboding, though it was seven o'clock in the morning. Usually the sun would be out and shining gloriously on summer mornings, but this was not the situation this morning. Without doubt, something unusual was going to happen this day. I saw Granny, my maternal grandmother, peering out of the window of her kitchen at the dark sky. I sensed that Granny was interested in the dark sky, because she gazed intently at it. Granny did not make any comments about the sky, though her face displayed some concern. Granny continued to prepare the early morning meal.

Aunt Linda, who is Granny's daughter and about ten years old, walked into the kitchen and remarked, "It is so dark this morning. I am going out to feed the chickens." Aunt Linda, who was dressed in a knee length dress, long cotton socks, and heavy shoes rushed out into the farm yard and coaxed the chickens out of their chicken house into the farm yard. Aunt Linda wore a pouch type apron around her waist, which was filled with cracked corn for the chickens. She tossed hands full of the corn from the apron onto the ground and the chickens pecked hurriedly at the corn and devoured it.

Granny was now tuning the old radio to another news channel. The radio announcer, who spoke rapidly, but at a normal tone of voice, described the weather conditions along the East Coast. He stated that a hurricane watch was in effect for eastern North Carolina and the panhandle. The announcer stated that Hurricane Donna would touch land at Wilmington, North Carolina and the surrounding counties early this evening. I raised my eyebrows and looked at Granny, who paused in her actions, to listen to the radio announcer's forecast. However, she only listened to the broadcast for a few seconds and was now cooking up eggs and other breakfast items for other family members.

Granny knew that the weather forecast would cause other family members, who lived up the dirt road a block from her house, to leave their shanties and trek up the road to visit Granny. Granny's house was always the main meeting place for our families or relatives. Our relatives could expect to eat a good home cook meal, compliments of Granny, when they arrived.

Granny then stated that storms are the Lord's work, because he created the heavens and the earth. We should not fear storms because everything that happens has a purpose and reason. Granny explained that the evil and wicked have reasons to fear storms because they do not live right in the eyes of the Lord. Therefore, they might perish without having obtained redemption. Granny often talked about religion and the need for people to be "saved" if they wanted to enter into God's Kingdom after their death. My relatives taught me when I was a child that heaven or God's Kingdom were paradise and the place to go after a person's death.

On the other hand, I was also told about hell and how mean and wicked people would suffer in hell forever after their deaths. I learned that going to hell would be an eternal stay or forever, once a person arrived there. I consider my family to be fairly religious. Therefore, I heard the older relatives warn us younger relatives about the discomforts of hell or burning in hell if we did not change our bad ways.

The warnings would cause my eyes to widen and fear would clutch at my heart. I had experienced extreme heat or high temperatures while harvesting crops in the fields of the farm, therefore thoughts of spending an eternity in hell were not refreshing. Thoughts of such a place sent shivers up and down my spine.

It never failed that people would use references of hell to make a point. I have heard children beg profusely for a toy or some other item while shopping with their parents. I have heard parents say, "Well people in hell want ice water and there is no chance that they will ever get ice water in hell." This comment normally got most children's attention and they stopped begging for a particular item. Comments such as this convinced me that I would be on my best behavior and evade the hot and fiery depths of hell where there is no ice water.

On occasions when I did some bad things, I would be frightened afterwards and pray for forgiveness. I could envision myself in hell and on a roasting spit over a roaring fire. I could imagine the odor of my burning flesh and singed hair wafting through the air. The hot North Carolina summers were unbearable, but I knew that fall, winter and spring would always come and give relief to the heat. In my opinion, hell, where there are supposedly severe summer conditions twenty-hours a day, is uninviting.

Uncle Leon appeared from a room where he had been sleeping. He was about fourteen years old and so full of life. There were no indications during his youth that during the years to come, as an adult, he would be killed in a tragedy. If this was a book of fiction or stories that I made up from my imagination, I could tailor the events to suit my needs. However, in the game of real life stories, a writer can only document the events in the manner that they occurred. Life is unpredictable. It reminds me of an old adage that I have often heard, "Here today, but gone tomorrow."

I then asked Granny and the other relatives about hurricanes. They explained that it was a bad storm with lots of rain and high winds and that on occasions, rural folk like us, would have to go to Wilmington or the city.

Wilmington was about ten miles from us and my older relatives explained that we could stay at a storm shelter there. Of course, my next question required my relatives to explain what a storm shelter was. I looked at them intently as they explained that the shelters were basements at the bottom of brick buildings or structures, which would withstand gale force, or terrific winds and turrets of rain. My eyes widened as my older relatives described the destructive force of hurricanes.

Cousin Howard, who was excited about the approaching storm, commented boldly that he was not personally concerned about the hurricane, as he munched vigorously on his breakfast foods. I noticed that Granny had served Cousin Howard a heaped plate of food and his slim frame was bent over his plate of food as he devoured it. Though Cousin Howard was only about nine years old, he stated boldly that storms were the Lord's work, therefore we should have no fear.

Uncle John had walked in to the house from inspecting the pigpen and other animal shelters. Uncle John glared at Cousin Howard and commented that Cousin Howard was running off at the mouth as usual. Cousin Howard paused in chewing his food. I saw a large lump of food slide down the front of his neck, headed toward his digestive tract. I heard Cousin Howard emit an audible gulp and a frown appeared on Cousin Howard's face. Given his quick temper, I was not surprised at his sudden remarks. Cousin Howard then raised his voice slightly and addressed all of us relatives present. He commented that he knew what he was talking about. I then saw Granny's brow slightly furrow. Before Uncle John could tell Cousin Howard that he did not know what he was talking about, which was a usual comment that Uncle John used in disagreements with other family members,

Granny told Cousin Howard to hush up and finish his breakfast. Cousin Howard was on the verge of grumbling out a comment but Granny's eyes flashed at him. Granny then playfully threatened Cousin Howard by stating " I will slap the tar out of you if you don't shut up." The conversation between Cousin Howard and Uncle John ended suddenly.

We other relatives then burst out with peals of laughter at Granny's comments, because she was comical in a serious way as always. However, we relatives always obeyed Granny's commands immediately, because any further outburst by a culprit would bring a volley of comments from Granny. Her comments were always similar to those of a Baptist preacher delivering a sermon of fire and brimstone to his parishioners. As devout Christians, comments about going to hell, if we did not abide by God's commandments and obey our elders, was a hair raising experience.

It seemed that during the nineteen fifties through nineteen seventies, people used fear as a tactic to keep unruly persons in line. One thing that instilled fear was corporal punishments. Adults used belts, straps, detachable electrical cords for irons, and paddles frequently on children to discipline them. Even the best-muscled buttocks were not invincible when the aforementioned instruments were wielded against them. The swats or strikes brought pain and it was not the same as jumping into cold water during a swim and adjusting to it. The additional swats of the paddle were always more painful than those that were first delivered, and no one could adjust to the pain. In the days of old it was a simple equation. Misdeeds equated to the presentation of a paddle and the painful application of it to the buttocks. The results were improved behavior on the part of the person punished.

When a paddle was produced, the eyes would widen and lock onto the instrument of pain. Pleading to escape the obvious never worked. This was also the situation at school and teachers wielded paddles like they were professional baseball players. Granted there were many buttocks available and it was a target rich environment, as an old clique goes.

At our junior high school, on occasions some privileged students would get to walk the "gauntlet" This was reserved for students that were either repeat offenders, who often broke school rules, or those who had done something awful enough to warrant suspension. A student was given the option of suspension or the gauntlet. The gauntlet consisted of about ten of the strongest teachers. They would stand five in a row side by side. Across from them would be five other teachers standing side by side and facing them. The student's objective was to start at one end of the gauntlet of teachers and walk through. However, he or she would stop at each teacher's position to receive a hard swat to the buttocks. The first swat was the tenderizer and everything went down hill from that point. Ten swats later, a student would be in severe pain and anguish. Word of the gauntlet flew like wildfire through the school in advance of the punishment. It sent shivers up the spines of the most incorrigible students and encouraged them to be more orderly in class. I guess incentive is the word to use here, because they gauntlet gave unruly students incentive to be on their best behavior.

The incidents of violence that have occurred in schools over the last twenty or so years were unheard of during the nineteen sixties and nineteen seventies, when corporal punishment was allowed in school systems.

There was dead silence for a moment, after Granny had admonished Snap, but within a few minutes us relatives began to discuss the storm again. All of my adult family members that were present decided that we would have to leave the family farm and venture to the city, where we would stay at a storm shelter during the hurricane.

Since the family had only one car, which Uncle John drove and two times more family members than what the car could hold, other forms of transportation to the city were discussed. The adults decided that the family would telephone for a taxicab. Granny had a telephone in her living room and a television in a den near the kitchen. A family member would use the telephone to summon a taxi. Granny then instructed family members to pack certain garments for our stay at the shelter. She also checked with Uncle John and Uncle Leon to insure that the livestock was secured as well as possible in their pens and properly fed.

I noticed that the sky over the farm was still very dark and menacing and the velocity of the wind had increased. The pine trees and bushes on and near the farm were swaying back and forth in unison like choreographed dancers and bending significantly while in motion.

Though it was now noontime, it appeared to be nightfall around the farm. This was not the best of situations and everyone seemed tense and worried except for Granny. In my opinion, Granny was fearless, because she had the strongest religious faith when compared to other people. It seemed that despite what might happen, good or bad, Granny's reservation in a better place was assured. Granny would often say, "You got to be right with God when your time comes. But since you do not know when that time might be, you got to be prepared at all times." Faith like Granny's could move mountains.

At about two o'clock in the evening that day, a family member summoned a taxicab by telephone. Upon arrival of the taxi, Uncle John followed the taxicab, with his Studebaker model car crammed full with our relatives. The taxicab was filled with other of our relatives also. It was now raining hard and rainwater was puddles on the highway, as we began our ten-mile trek to the city or Wilmington, North Carolina. The wind blew hard and the taxicab in which I rode was buffeted back and forth by the wind. The taxi swayed from side to side and up and down, like a boat in a choppy ocean. The sky was pitch black as night, though it was only about three o'clock in the afternoon. The wind continued to howl and moan like a pack of wild dogs or wolves.

Trees swayed violently from left to right, but the worst of the storm was yet to come. My eyes were wide with fear and my heartbeat had increased. My relatives and I began to make remarks about the intensity of the wind and rain.

I will always remember an old adage, "United we stand. Divided We Fall." With my relatives accompanying me in the taxicab, I felt comfort, because they were fearless people in many ways. My relatives were strong in body from the harsh farm work that they endured and strong in their beliefs of the heavenly father and believed in a spiritual life after death. For them, the storm was a challenge of their Christian beliefs. I remember from the bible a particular scripture. I will paraphrase it. It reads that though I walk through the valley of the shadow of death, I shall fear no evil because God is with me. In our hearts and minds, our faith in God was strong as we rode towards the storm shelter.

Our thoughts were also on the family members that had stayed behind. Aunt Peggy with her son, Howard, and Aunt Margaret with her sons William and Earl had decided to weather the storm in their large shanty. Trees surrounded their shanty. The trees were far from their shanty and would not pose a danger. The trees would also serve as barriers when the gale force winds arrived later that evening. Aunt Peggy and Aunt Margaret were both steadfast individuals. They made the decision to weather the storm at home and Granny did not encourage them to do otherwise. Both of my aunts were unmovable mountains and nothing seemed to frighten them. Of course, Aunt Margaret was a powerhouse of a woman and stood near six feet tall. When she wore certain hairstyles, she reminded me of some of Japan's top sumo wrestlers. On occasions, the unwise would engage Aunt Margaret in a battle of the words. They learned too late that she possessed a sharp tongue and superior brawn to back up her words.

Aunt Margaret also had a taste for certain foods or delicacies and Aunt Peggy was no slouch in that department either. Aunt Peggy was famous for saying, "Hmmmm, that was delicious" after eating most foods. I will be honest and say that everyone in my family has great appetites. I did find Aunt Margaret's tastes for certain foods to be a bit more extravagant than most of us relatives.

On occasions, I would see Aunt Margaret with a snapping turtle and it would be rather large. In one hand, Aunt Margaret would have a hatchet and in the other a wire clothes hanger. She would poke the end of the clothes hanger at the turtle's mouth and true to its name, the turtle's mouth and jaws would snap down onto the end of the clothes hanger, which was fashioned into a hook at the end. The turtle's mouth would be snared on the hook of the clothes hanger and Aunt Margaret would struggle to pull its head away from the shell and extend the neck for a fatal blow. The powerful turtle would try to retract its head and close the shell to protect its head, however it would be no match for Aunt Margaret's strength. She would extend the head and neck from the turtle's shell and then raise the hatchet far above her head for a fatal blow to the turtle's neck. Aunt Margaret would then use the hatchet to remove the turtle from its armored shell and then prepare its remains for her fabulous turtle stew.

I would watch the whole affair at some distance. Aunt Margaret would glance at me from time to time as she prepared the turtle outside of her shanty. When I was an adolescent, I was in awe of Aunt Margaret's size and strength. Therefore, I always kept my distance from her.

After Aunt Margaret prepared the turtle for cooking, she would take it inside of the shanty for stewing. She would add various spices and vegetables with the turtle meat. Someone might get a taste for turtle stew, which people boasts tastes like a combination of chicken, seafood, beef and other meats. I must warn that there are certain portions of a turtle that must be discarded during preparation. If not discarded, someone will develop some serious stomach problems or worst. I would advise that anyone having a taste for turtle, to consult with people who know how to prepare them or buy the meat inspected and prepared for consumption.

When Aunt Margaret would go into her shanty to cook the turtle, I would wait about twenty minutes to ensure that she was fully occupied. I would then move slowly towards her shanty and to where the decapitated head of the turtle laid on the ground. I picked up a stick and poked at the head of the turtle. I was startled when the eyes of the severed head blinked open and the mouth snapped at me.

I was careful not to poke my finger at the turtle's head. I had heard stories that once a snapping turtle got a hold of your finger that he would not let it go until it thundered. I figured that this could be a problem if there was no forecast of a thunderstorm for days to come. I heard that some people would bang on a metal wash pan to simulate thunder and the turtle would then release the person's finger.

I fiddled around with the severed head for several minutes and then snuck off to play in a stream of water near our shanty. Two hours later, I returned to the severed head and the eyes and mouth still moved. Three hours after the turtle's demise, I was crouching at a distance and saw Aunt Margaret throw some bones into the refuse can, which is what remained of the turtle. She had already devoured a portion of the turtle. Five hours after the turtle's demise, I check the severed head and the responses were minimal. I have often imagined that I would have done well in the field of medicine because I was a keen observer back then. Finally, six hours after the turtle's demise, I noted no reactions as I prodded the severed head. It was interesting that the head had survived to witness both the turtle's death and its consumption as the main course.

I have run into some folks from Louisiana, and they rave about turtle stew and how the turtle tastes like a combination of various meats. Well, I never had a taste for turtle and never ate any. Nor do I have any aspirations about eating turtle in the future.

Well, let me get back to the story about the storm. As we rode toward the storm shelter at Wilmington, Granny made a few comments about Aunt Margaret and Aunt Peggy's decision to weather the storm at home with their sons. Granny felt that it was not the wisest decision to weather the storm at their house, but she respected her daughters' decision. With a determined but solemn look on her countenance, Granny concluded that the situation was now in God's hands and she would pray for her daughters and their sons' safety.

Forty-five years later, when I was almost fifty years old, I had attended funerals of many relatives during my lifetime. I have come to certain conclusions about life and death. There is an old adage that states, "Tomorrow is promised to no one", therefore I thrive to live my life to the fullest. I am better able nowadays to appreciate Granny's thoughts concerning her daughter's decisions. Nowadays, I notice that people are concerned about their children and relatives who perform military duties in war stricken areas worldwide. Unfortunately, some of the soldiers sometime return stateside to attend the funerals of relatives that were killed by violence or accidents here in the United States.

I am simply making the point that people should not worry excessively about situations. People must consider that they can be called home at any time, whether we are at home lounging in front of the television or in a war stricken area of the world. People should have a concern about being prepared for death when it summons them. I believe that death is often caused by a series of events. People through various actions set events into motion that will cause their deaths or the deaths of others. However, there are things that can intercede into certain events and prevent death or serious injury.

I recall during nineteen seventy-four, I was stationed as a soldier in West Germany and met a vivacious lady, who was a few years older than me.

One day, I was walking with the lady and her toddler son in the crowded downtown area of Stuttgart, Germany. Streetcars on rails crisscrossed the cobblestone streets of the downtown district. My girlfriend and her son were walking ahead of me and failed to notice that a streetcar was approaching them from the left. They walked forward into the path of the oncoming streetcar and were not alert to its approach because of its quiet electric engines. I saw that their deaths were imminent and grasped them both by the shoulders, which prevented the fatal collision.

If I had not met the lady weeks earlier, would she and her son have perished that day under the weight of the streetcar? However, we must consider that since I only visited her on the weekends, would she have been visiting or traveling elsewhere, instead of staying at home for my weekend visit. Of course, she could have been traveling or visiting somewhere else and could have had an unfortunate accident or tragedy there.

I believe that sometimes in the game of life, one should not examine the possibilities or scenarios, but accept the tragedy or misfortune. After entertaining several arguments, one can safely conclude that my girlfriend and her son were careless when they crossed the street. The presence of several streetcars in the downtown district would have caused a person to be more cautious as a pedestrian.

Of course, there is the issue of pedestrians or motorists who looked in various directions to insure that it was clear before crossing but were involved in accidents for failing to yield the right of way. They looked but did not see the oncoming vehicles. I have found from my personal experiences that my brain concludes the coast is clear, though my eyes see that there are immediate dangers. This is caused by inattention or daydreaming. I use the "look a second time" method before entering the flow of traffic or changing lanes. This method has saved me from numerous deadly collisions. I am saying that we do have control over our destinies if we are careful and prudent in our day-to-day affairs.

We continued to towards the storm shelter. The gale force winds whispered and howled loudly and blew torrents of rain across the roadway. We noticed that there were no cars with headlights headed towards the rural county that we had just departed. Our ten-mile drive to town seemed like an eternity and I was slightly frightened by the storm or hurricane. This was the first hurricane that I had witnessed during my lifetime. But later while living in the coastal town of Wilmington, I would experience several more hurricanes. The storm seemed relentless. I could see destruction in its wake as large trees lay fallen and uprooted upon the ground and tree leaves lay in piles near the roadway.

We arrived at the storm shelter, which was located in the basement of a brick two-story building. Military style foldout cots were arranged in neat rows on the floor of the shelter or basement. Some people were either sitting on the cots and engaged in hushed conversations or lying on the cots. There was a counter, on which refreshments were neatly displayed, and an attendant was handing out blankets to people staying at the shelter. Though we were below ground level, in the storm shelter, I could still hear the muffled howling of the wind and the monotonous tapping noise of the heavy rain against the exterior of the shelter. It was slightly dark in the shelter but there was enough lighting to see walkways and other people milling about. My relatives and I were grouped together on cots and Granny had some fried chicken and other convenient foods in a container. It was about four o'clock in the evening and we ate a small snack while awaiting the serving of the evening meal at the shelter.

Our trip to the storm shelter was perhaps the second time that my relatives had left their small farm as a group. During nineteen fifty-seven, within weeks after the killing of my paternal grandmother by Pa Daddy, Granny, her children and grandchildren departed the small farm. My mother, my siblings and I were with our relatives when they departed the farm. We traveled to Granny's ancestral home, which was in another county about thirty miles from Granny and Pa Daddy's small farm. This was the county where Granny and her six siblings were reared by her parents. Granny and her siblings were born between the end of the nineteenth century (1890) and the beginning of the twentieth century (1905). It is safe to assume that my Granny's grandparents were born before the end of slavery or 1863, which was the signing of the Emancipation Proclamation by Abraham Lincoln.

Granny's parents, her grandparents and great grand parents were farmers and acquired farmland in Pender County, North Carolina at the end of the enslavement of Black people in America. My family has kept ownership of our farmland for about one hundred and forty years. Our family belief about ownership of farmland is, "Our farmland can be sold only to blood relatives." When Granny's parents died, they split up the parent's land among the children. Granny received a sizeable acreage of land as her inheritance. Some of Granny's inheritance was cleared farmland and some was covered with trees and brush.

Granny and us relatives decided to leave our small farm, because Uncle John had felt that relatives of my father would attack our family. Supposedly, there was a rumor that my father's family wanted revenge for Pa Daddy killing my paternal grandmother. Uncle John discussed the issue with Granny and they decided that the family would leave the farm and venture to Granny's ancestral home where two of her brothers and two sisters resided. Granny rented the farm, which included her house to some tenants. Granny loved her house and farm, therefore this was one of the most difficult decisions that she ever made during her lifetime.

Granny and our relatives lived with her sisters and brothers in their homes for a few months and moved back to the family farm. Though blood relatives always extend their hospitality, over time, living with others can become a cramped arrangement.

One of Granny's brothers was infamous for playing an honesty game with my younger aunts and uncle who were barely in their teens. He would leave fruits and sweets on a dining table so that his nephews and nieces could see them. No one would touch the items and within a short time later, the uncle would comment that no one had touched the fruits and sweets. He would further comment that he had left the fruits and sweets on the dining table for his sister's children to eat. My uncle and aunts would then eat the fruits and sweets. Within a short time later, or the next day, they would see more fruits and sweets displayed on the table. My uncles and aunts would consume the items, but their uncle would become upset and comment that they ate the items without asking. He would scold them and remind them about the rules of honesty. I chuckled

en Aunt Virginia told me this story about this
rticular uncle or great uncle. I know the story is
rue because some people never change peculiar
things about themselves over time.

My brother George and I had an encounter
with this particular great uncle during a visit to his
home. Pear and peach trees and farmland
surrounded his house. His homestead was well
maintained like my other relatives who farmed the
land in that area or county. George and I spied
several bushels of peaches and pears on back of the
great uncle's pick up truck. We decided that we
would sample the bounty of fruit so amply
displayed before us. Surely, no one would mind,
since there was so much in abundance, and the trees
nearby were also heavily laden with fruit. As we
munched on the succulent peaches and pears, we
were under the surveillance of our great uncle. He
was peering through a window with a slight smile
on his countenance. He knew that the display of
fruit on his truck was tempting, but according to the
rules of honesty, my brother and I had stolen the
fruit. We did not ask permission to eat the fruit.

An hour later, we bounced into the great
uncle's house to drink some cool well water. The
great uncle commented that though he had fruit in
abundance on his truck, it is always necessary to ask
for things that do not belong to you. George and I
hung our heads in shame, because we had been
caught red handed or stealing. I then told my great
uncle that my brother and I would pick two bushels
of fruit from the trees to atone for our sin. Our great

uncle smiled broadly and was happy with that arrangement. Our encounter with this particular uncle placed credence in the story that Aunt Virginia had told me about him and the honesty game that he played.

Though I am about fifty years old nowadays, I still remember the encounter with this particular great uncle, though he is deceased. Granted he had the upper hand in the honesty game that he played with adolescent members of our family, but the righteous always hold the upper hand. I am glad that I was receptive of the guidance that this great uncle provided, because some young people nowadays rebel at authority and guidance. In the short run, these rebellious youth find themselves incarcerated and realize too late that someone really cared about them. If only they had listened.

When Granny and our relatives returned to their farm, they found it somewhat ill kept but still standing. They cleaned the farmhouse and repaired fencing. Granny was now back home and would never leave her home again during her lifetime.

It was about seven o'clock the next morning after the storm had subsided and we were allowed to depart the shelter. Tree leaves covered the city streets of Wilmington and torrents of rainwater were flowing along the culverts of the city streets into sewer drains.

The sun was beaming in the sky and the temperature was about seventy-five degrees, therefore it was fairly warm outside. Granny praised God for sparing and preserving us during the storm.

.iced that the faces of my relatives beamed with
ppiness because the severe storm had passed. I
so noticed a large radiant blue, yellow, and red
rainbow in the sky. Some of my relatives reminded
each other to make a wish. I was told that a pot of
gold was buried in the ground at the end of the
rainbow. After I asked several childish questions
about the rainbow and gold, it was explained that
the pot of gold is a myth. It seemed to me that it
would be impossible to find the end of the rainbow,
because it was so massive and seemed to stretch on
forever across the sky.

In my opinion, a rainbow is hope and
emphasizes that we should believe in our creator.
Perhaps, at the end of the rainbow there is eternal
life or a place of peace. Perhaps it symbolizes the
long journey that we will make during a lifetime and
the end of the rainbow is the reward for living a
righteous life.

When we arrived back at the family farm later
that morning, it seemed that the house, the animal
pens and other structures had been power washed
clean. Everything was sparkling clean. I looked
upon the sky and its horizons and noticed that they
were a magnificent blue color. Yes, the destructive
storm was gone, but our farm suffered no damages
and no loss of farm life. Aunt Margaret and Aunt
Peggy with their sons also survived the storm and
their shanty and my mother's shanty were not
damaged. Granny commented that we would thank
God, because through our prayers, he spared our
farm. Granny explained that she had prayed and that

her prayers were fulfilled. I looked upon Granny countenance or face and it was filled with gladness and appreciation.

Granny was never a very wealthy woman in regards to personal belongings but she owned more land than any average American and saved more money than the average person. However, despite what she owned, Granny was rich with the blessings of the creator. She would live to be over one hundred years old and was rarely sick or ambulatory over the years. Granny would prepare meals up to the day of her death. I feel that people should cherish life and good health instead of material possessions, because what good are possessions when you are frequently ill or feeling pains.

It is often said that home is where the heart is. Years later when Granny would be about eighty years old, someone would give her a small-furnished trailer home. The trailer was parked at the rear of Granny's old farmhouse and it was more comfortable and presentable then Granny's old house. However, Granny never lived in the trailer home. We relatives would see Granny exit the rear door of her house and walk a short distance to the trailer home and enter it. Granny would walk through the trailer and look at its nice furniture and cabinets with a slight smile on her face. She would laugh slightly to herself and shake her head in wonder. Granny would seemly remark. "A nice trailer home, but no place nicer than my old house, not even the world's prettiest castles."

Within a year or two, Granny lost interest in the trailer home and got rid of it. I guess life that way sometime. We admire nice things, but after we possess them, nice things don't mean much anymore and we seem to lose interest in them.

I will always believe that we rural folks have always loved the land and rural areas. All you need in the country is a suitable house or shanty to sleep in. The virtual untouched beauty of nature in the rural areas or country is always a draw to most folks, even those who live in the city. Being in the country and living in an inexpensive house is good living in my opinion.

I can imagine right now walking up a country road to the creek with a fishing pole in one hand and a cooler of soft drinks in the other. Of course, a good sandwich or two in the cooler would be a great snack while fishing.

I had witnessed the destructive forces of nature the day before, but the next day, I witnessed the calm and serenity of nature. Without doubt, nature is beautiful and peaceful the majority of the time, but it often give us early warnings about its destructive forces. Then we can prepare ourselves for nature's storms.

We should compare nature with our day-to-day lives. Because in the game of life there will be mostly good times, but there will be some turbulent times also. We can prepare ourselves for the turbulent times of life by acquiring a religious faith and adhering to it when the turbulent times occur.

So, we were back at our farm the next day, which we had left the day before, in the wake of a storm. My grandmother prayed the day of the storm, for the preservation of the farm, which is what we saw the next day upon our return. It really shows that with prayer and faith we can influence the circumstances of our destinies.

Over twenty years ago, I decided to create a poem to celebrate nature, but I wanted nature to be portrayed with human qualities or what is called personification. I believe you will enjoy the following poem.

The Painter

He stood with shoulders hunched,
Spying upon a morning sun,
With a face slightly crinkled.
He stood unmoving,

In clothes soiled and fiercely wrinkled,
And upon feet that strode,
Brown shoes rusty and crinkled.
Saying to self,

Thus a fine day for changes of,
All things ugly and drab,
That taints the earth ground.
Picking up paints and brushes,

He strode bowlegged forth,
On shoes that groaned,

And seemly moaned,
With a face that seemed aloft.

He spied upon the skies and horizons,
With sudden interest in eye.
Selecting a frosty blue,
He proceeded to paint the sky.

Until……..
The sky had its fill.
He looked upon all things green,
With yellows, reds and gold,

He painted all the leaves.
The painter strode towards the sea,
Disturbing resting seagulls,
Who fluttered and screeched,
At this indignity.

Selecting a dark blue green,
He proceeded to paint the sea,
With a glint of steel in eye,
Until the sea had its fill.

Feeling a sudden chill with dread,
Turning about he fled,
Stumbling and falling in crooked shoes,
Tearing things asunder.

In some place far he stopped,
And looked with interest all about.
Yellows, reds, and gold,

Work for days untold.

I looked out of the window of Granny's hou~
during that evening, a day after that terrible storm.
The sun was sitting low in the western skies. Soon
the darkness of the night would come and another
day would be over.

But tomorrow would be another day. My eyes
will see the rising of the morning sun. I will bask in
its warmth. I will run towards the sun with my arms
flung wide, with the wind ripping through my
clothes and hair. It is so great to be alive.

CHAPTER SIX

Harvesting the River

We would often walk up the railroad track for about a mile to a small tributary of a river that was located below the Railroad Bridge. We call the Railroad Bridge a trussell. The large pond below the trussell or Railroad Bridge was fed by the large Cape Fear River, which ran a considerable number of miles along the Eastern Shore of North Carolina. Like an octopus, narrow arms of water extended from the large Cape Fear River and fed into large tributaries or ponds of water. This is how the large pond of water below the Railroad Bridge came into being. The pond was filled with fresh water trout and catfish. The fish were bountiful.

Aunt Virginia, Aunt Della, Aunt Linda and Uncle Leon, who were my youngest aunts and uncle and were five to fifteen years older than me. They would escort Cousin Howard, Cousin William, Helen (my sister), George (my brother), and me to the pond below the railroad bridge. We would march down the railroad tracks to the pond.

I would play a game of leaping from one railroad wooden tire or wooden support beam, which the shiny metal train rails were attached, to another adjacent beam. Underneath the shiny railroad rails and wooden support beams was gravel or rocks. It intrigued me how the railroad tracks were laid out for miles and miles. It seemed that the rails went on forever and did not end.

On both sides of the railway at a distance were the woods or large quantities of pine trees. North Carolina is often called the "Tar Heel State" because the pine trees during the hot summer months would ooze out sticky tarry syrup onto the ground. If a person stepped too close to a pine tree during the summer time, he or she would step on tar from the tree and it would stick to their shoes or feet. It took some effort to remove the tree tar from one's feet or shoes. Thus the name "Tar Heel State" originated from the tar that the pine trees secreted.

Because the tree line was a considerable distance from the railroad tracks, we were afforded no shade from the sun. The hot sun during the summer months would beam down unmercifully on our heads and shoulders. Often we wore wide brim straw hats to deflect the harmful rays of the sun.

Often, we would see either freight trains or passenger trains chugging along the railroad tracks. We smaller children would wave vigorously at the train conductor and his crew, who worn denim hats and denim coveralls. The train crew never disappointed us. They would always throw hands full of candy to us as the trains passed my maternal grandparents small farm. The train rails were located about forty feet from the front of the farm, but the rails were lower in elevation than out farm. A ditch with a flowing stream of water was near the rails.

During the early 1960s, I would see the cars of the passenger trains loaded up with soldiers as the

enger trains sped past our farm. I was told that
diers riding in the train were headed to the war in
ietnam. I was so proud to see American soldiers
on their way to battle.

I would be confused later when I saw people
protesting the war. As I grew older, I would learn
more about the war in Vietnam. I would volunteer
for military service during nineteen seventy-four,
when our soldiers were still in Vietnam, but our
military was not dispatching any more soldiers there
for duty. In fact, within a year or so after I enlisted
for military service, our soldiers would be taken out
of Vietnam.

The War in Vietnam or Police Action, as it
was commonly referred to, is now history. Our
military would get a lot of bad press about the War
in Vietnam, but during the 1980s, after the Invasion
of Grenada, West Indies, our military would be
exonerated in the eyes of the public in regards to the
Vietnam War, which we neither lost nor won in a
sense. Shortly thereafter, veterans of Vietnam
marched proudly in national parades and were
cheered by huge crowds. It had taken over a decade
for America to receive them home from the
Vietnam War with loving arms, but what a welcome
it was. I hope that this country never again forsakes
it soldiers and military people.

I know in my heart that some of the soldiers
that I saw riding on the passenger train as it passed
our small farm, died in Vietnam and did not make it
home alive. I can only conclude that a soldier goes
where his or her country or government sends him

or her. However, that same government must be the responsibility for sending its soldiers into an unjust war and insure that they are treated with respect and dignity upon their return.

I got a little sidetracked while reminiscing about the trains and the railroad near our farm. But I had to mention the brave soldiers who served in Vietnam. It goes to show that a train goes down a railroad track for many reasons. Sometimes to haul freight and cargo, but sometimes to take people far from home. I can still remember seeing them proud and brave soldiers waving at me when I was wee lad dressed in denim clothing with a fat cap on my head. I will never forget them. Of course, they threw lots of candy to my cousins and me. The candy was always delicious.

We would walk about a mile before we came to the Railroad Bridge. There was a large pond of bluish green water below it. The bridge was about twenty feet above the pond. We would then slide down a grassy and hilly slope at the beginning of the Railroad Bridge until we were standing at the edge of the pond. We would see bubbles from fish surfacing to the top of the sparkling pond. One could see his or her reflection on the shiny surface of the pond. However, on this very hot and humid summer's day during August 1960, something strange had occurred.

The hot summer with only a few rain showers had failed to maintain the water level of the Cape Fear River and it tributaries. Therefore, no water had flowed into the pond to replenish it, and the

level was very low. Normally the water level
ld be about eight feet deep in the pond but on
is particular day the water level was a mere two to
nree feet deep. Near the edges of the pond, fish
were visible and we were able to walk into the pond
and pick up the fish with our hands. Immediately,
one of my aunts dispatched an older cousin to return
to the farm and notify other relatives of our good
fortune. The cousin was instructed to tell other
family members to come to the pond with large
fifty-gallon tin tubs.

My aunts, uncle, my siblings and I began to
scoop up the fish from the pond by hand and string
them onto a piece of fishing line by pushing a piece
of wood attached to the fishing line into the fish's
mouth. Once the stick, with a fishing line attached,
was pushed inside of a fish's mouth, we would
angle the stick so it would come out the side of the
fish's head through its gills. We would then take the
same length of stick and string another fish onto the
same portion of fishing line until we had about one
hundred fish attached to fishing line by their gills.
We then placed all of the fish on the fishing line into
the pond's water to keep them alive until we were
ready and able to transport them home.

Within thirty minutes, several of my older
aunts and Uncle John arrived with several fifty-
gallon tin tubs. Some of us resembled grizzly bears
as we waded in water just below our knees and
scooped up wiggling and tail splashing fresh water
trout with out hands. Some of my relatives had worn
sturdy work gloves and were also able to catch some

catfish to add to the larger variety of trout. Gran had a large deep freezer at home and upon her arrival at the pond, she remarked that other relative could label their catch with their names on freezer bags and most of the fish would be frozen for our later consumption. Granny estimated that we would freeze enough fish to last throughout the summer and winter. I already knew what was going to be on that evening's menu, fried fish. I could smell (envisioning) the rich full aroma of frying fish wafting through the breezy air at the pond.

Needless to say, the drought was beneficial in an odd way, because the 1950s and 1960s were economical bad times for most families in the rural south. My maternal grandfather or Pa Daddy was absent, which meant that the family income was reduced. I had never seen Pa Daddy and only knew that on occasions he mailed my grandmother, his wife, hand weaved pocketbooks. I did not know of his whereabouts and as a five-year-old, Pa Daddy's whereabouts was not important to me.

I also knew that I had a father, who would visit my mother and us siblings at the farm on a few occasions. My father, William, was a short and slight built man but he had muscular arms and legs and certain strength about himself. I noticed that during my father's visits to our shanty from 1960 to 1961, he seemed sad and reserved. I found his eyes remarkable because they seemed quick and intelligent during conversations he had with my mother during his few visits.

Though I was five and then six years old

g his visits from 1960 to 1961, it seemed that father was a man who had lived a rigorous life. **ut** it seemed that he had a considerable weight on **his** shoulders. A voice within his soul sometimes announced that he had lost something of significance to him during his lifetime. I would sometimes see my father over the years silently suffering over something that seemed to be ripping his inner being apart. However, it was seldom that I would see him that way. But often he would smile during his hard moments, and remark that life is short and that people should live it to the fullest.

My father and mother separated for four years during 1957, which was the year that Pa Daddy accidentally killed my father's mother.

I would be told about my family's awful secret when I turned thirteen years old. Then my earlier observations of many seemly strange things prior to the revealing of the secret would come full circle. I would come to know about the awful burden that my family carried and why my father would sometimes have unprovoked and short periods of anger and frustration.

After we scooped hundreds of fish out of the pond by hand, and placed them in large metal wash pans, we began our hike back to the farm. Since the pans were heavy with fish and pond water, which kept the fish alive, we took turns lifting and carrying the pans.

About thirty minutes after we began our return trip laden with fish, we arrived back at the farm. The majority of the fish were placed in large freezer bags and placed in Granny's large deep freezer, which was located inside of a storage house. Aunt Peggy and Aunt Margaret lived in a large shanty about one city block from Granny's farm house and about one hundred feet next to their shanty was a shanty where my mother (Annie), my sister (Helen), my brother (George) and I lived. My Uncle John, who is my mother's brother, built our shanty for two hundred dollars. Aunt Peggy had one son (Howard) who was about four years older than me. Aunt Margaret had two sons (William and Earl). Cousin Earl was the same age as me. Cousin William was two years old than me. Cousin William's nickname was Bubba. I guess this name was appropriate for him, because he was taller and bigger than the other boy cousins.

I will always give thanks for the many fish that we harvested from the pond. It was a miracle in a sense. But then miracles occurred at Granny's house often. It seemed that Granny could feed our relatives by the hundreds and her provisions of food never dwindled. Granny could have ten relatives show up on a Sunday unannounced and she would cook more to accommodate them. However, before suppertime was over, a total of thirty relatives would be at her modest farmhouse. Within minutes she would have cooked even more food to feed such a large crowd of relatives. My relatives often were in awe as to how Granny accomplished such feats. It seemed like magic.

I was determined to learn Granny's secrets in feeding large crowds of relatives at record speeds. I

...rned that Granny had a variety of vegetables, ...ome precooked, frozen in freezer bags in her deep ...freezer. She also had precut portions of meat frozen in the same manner. A pot filled with hot water and a large frying pan with heated grease were items that Granny used in her hasty preparation of more food for additional relatives. I also learned that meats like ground beef and pork could be expanded in volume with a hand full of flour tossed into a bowl of meat. No one would notice that the meat was part flour, because the largest percentage of the mix was meat. People who cooked back during the 1950s and 1960s were masters of substitution.

I still love the hot dog relish that Paul's Place, an eatery near Castle Hayne, North Carolina places on its hotdogs. The relish has an historical significance because during World War II, meat was rationed. The American soldiers fighting in the war needed meat products and a significant amount of it was shipped to Europe for the military's use. Americans were given rationed amounts of meat per family and ration coupons allowed them to purchase only a specific amount.

Paul's Place concocted a relish from vegetables to replace chili, which was made of meat, because the rationing limited making chili. The restaurant then heated the relish like it was chili. It became so popular that patrons did not want to switch back to chili concocted from meat after World War II ended. Therefore, if you visit Paul's Place today, you will have an opportunity to eat some of the world's tastiest hotdogs with a chili substitute or vegetable relish.

I will always have mostly fond memories of the past. In my opinion, life was better during my younger days. As a child, I did not have the responsibilities that I have nowadays as an adult. The past is very relative to how we live today during the present time. Sometimes, life was hard or difficult during the past. But the harshness of life back then, is what motivates me nowadays to succeed or excel.

I can only sigh now, and with a bemused expression on my face, I can envision events from the past. It is like sitting in a movie theater and looking at the previews, but they are of past events.

I am forty-nine years old nowadays. I will now take a refreshing nap on my comfortable recliner. And if Death comes, it will not catch me flat on my back, so to speak. I believe that you can always fight better sitting up than lying down. Someday, Death will be the clear winner in the trials of my life, but it will know that it had been in a fight. Nope, I am not going without a fight.

CHAPTER SEVEN

Our Little Shanty

During the summer of nineteen sixty, my mother returned home from the hospital. I had only vague memories of her because I was only four years old when she was placed in the hospital. Despite the situation, I recognized my mother when she walked into my Granny's house. Granny was very happy that my mother had returned from the hospital, because she smiled broadly and greeted my mother, Annie. The majority of my relatives were present when my mother returned and they greeted her heartily also.

I noticed that Aunt Margaret, who was the oldest and the largest of my mother's sisters looked at my mother but paused before greeting her. It always seemed that Aunt Margaret was always reserved when greeting or speaking with other relatives and people that she met. It always seemed that Aunt Margaret knew something of interest about most people she spoke with, whether it was good or bad. I can remember even today the way in which Aunt Margaret glanced at my other siblings and me. Her glance seemed to convey concern, because she was a keeper of my family's dreadful secret or tragedy that had occurred on the family farm during nineteen fifty-seven. Realistically, my siblings and I were a burden, because of the tragedy. However, none of my relatives ever stated that we were a burden.

When my mother was in the hospital, Aunt Virginia was the surrogate or stand in mother for my brother and me. My sister, Helen, was two years older than I during the year nineteen sixty. Helen was seven years old and attending elementary school. Helen was old enough to know who our mother was. Therefore she did not bond with her younger aunts in a motherly way like my brother and I. Aunt Virginia was perhaps fifteen years old when she filled in as my surrogate mother. I used to call her mother, but she reminded me who my mother was and that she was my aunt. Even today, I have a special relationship with Aunt Virginia because she was my stand in mother during my adolescence, when my mother was hospitalized.

Granny worked part time doing housework for well to do white folk in the farming community. The extra money that Granny earned helped buy food for her children and a host of grandchildren. Granny never turned any relative away from her door to conserve food.

Living on the small farm had its advantages. We had livestock to slaughter for food and grew more vegetables than we could eat. Granny would also buy peaches and pears by the bushel. She and her daughters would partially cook the fruits and vegetables and vacuum seal them in glass Mason Jars with lids for later consumption. The jars filled with hot partially cooked fruits and vegetables were placed in a galvanized tub of hot water. The lids of the jars were screwed on tightly to create a ssurized seal. This preservation technique is lled **canning**. The sealed jars or fruits and vegetables would retain their freshness for years after the jars were pressure sealed. My favorite desert was hot home made biscuits with peaches from the Mason Jars.

In reality, my family, immediate and extended were a corporation. We worked together to run the farm even during the absence of my maternal grandfather, who my relatives called "Muh Daddy", which is the pronunciation for "My Daddy".

I noticed while growing up that we folks from the rural south had our own pronunciation or slang for some things. Our pronunciation would sometimes confuse people, who either resided in the urban or city areas of North Carolina, or people who originated from other states.

In the previous editions of this book, my paternal grandfather is referred to as "Pa Daddy." "Pa Daddy" and "Muh Daddy" were slang names for my maternal grandfather. I would often listen to Cousin Howard talk about "Pa Daddy" and he would always say that things at the farm would change when "Pa Daddy" returned. Perhaps Cousin Howard was saying "Muh Daddy" during his conversations with me, but it sounded like "Pa Daddy" to me. This is often the problem with slang, because pronunciations of certain words can be confusing to the listener, who then creates yet another modified pronunciation for a word. After the first edition of this book was published, Aunt

Virginia contacted me and explained the conflict. I thanked her, but commented that "Pa Daddy" seemed more appropriate for my maternal grandfather, because he was not "my daddy" but my granddaddy.

After my mother's return, she worked for some time at a café located adjacent to a major rural highway and about three miles from our family farm. We considered three miles as walking distance. Modern transportation has spoiled us humans, because nowadays some people will not walk four blocks to travel to a store.

My mother contracted with Uncle John, her brother to build her a two-room shanty on a portion of Aunt Peggy's land. My mother paid Uncle John $200.00 to build the small shanty and it was adjacent to Aunt Peggy's larger shanty, which she shared with Aunt Margaret and her two sons. Most people would consider us poor. However, when I moved to the nearby city when I was six years old, I would find most of my peers living in rented houses. In my family's opinion, ownership of a house represented wealth instead of renting.

I would run up the dirt road that connected my grandparents, Aunt Peggy's shanty, and our shanty, which was under construction. I would see Uncle John and his younger brother, Uncle Leon building our shanty from the ground up. Our shanty had wooden walls and a tin roof. The shanty also had a hole cut in one wall (fireproofed), through which a galvanized stovepipe sheath was installed. The metal stovepipe sheath would allow the hookup a wood stove so that smoke from burning wood would escape through the improvised chimney to the exterior of the house. I would stand and admire my uncles building the shanty and they would yell, "Hi there Willie" and I would greet them in return. My relatives were often very sociable with each other and greeted each other with smiles and pleasantries.

After several days of sawing wood and pounding nails, my mother's new shanty was ready for occupation. The shanty had two large rooms and one large room was for sleeping. My uncles placed a large bed in one of the rooms. My mother and we three siblings slept in the same bed. My older sister slept at the foot of the bed. My brother and I slept with our mother at the head of the bed. A year later, my mother would place another bed in the second room and she would sleep in it alone

There was a large table in the adjacent or second room. A two-burner kerosene-cooking stove sat on top of the table. My mother prepared our meals on the stove and later she purchased a portable oven that sat over the flame of the kerosene stove. My mother would mix flour, baking soda, and salt to create homemade biscuits, which she would cook in the oven. The nineteen fifties were a time or era of simplicity. A gallon of kerosene cost about five cents and gasoline was about ten cents a gallon. Therefore, cooking on the kerosene stove was an inexpensive way to prepare meals. Creating an oven to sit on top of the kerosene stove was very innovative, but a creation of simplicity also. The

kerosene stove was efficient and always worked, b
a negative side effect was the noxious fumes of
burning kerosene that emitted from it when the
burners were ignited. It was always wise to raise the
windows for ventilation when operating the
kerosene stove.

On occasions, my mother would heat a black
metal straightening comb over the flames of the
kerosene stove. She would place promenade or hair
grease in my sister's hair and use the heated metal
comb to straighten the kinks out of my sister's hair.
My sister, Helen, would often brawl or cry because
my mother would tug on the comb to pull it through
the coarsest hair on my sister's head. The whole
affair seemed comical to me, and I would suppress
myself from laughing. I was happy that as a boy
child, I did not possess a head full of hair that
needed weekly attention.

Of course, no house or shanty is complete
without a source of heat for the cold winter days.
There was a galvanized steel or tin wood burning
stove situated in the large room that we used for
sleeping. The stove's exterior would be cherry red
when we placed large amounts of wood in it to heat
the cold and drafty shanty during the winter.

We lived a Spartan existence because there
was very little furnishing in the shanty. We had an
eating table that had about sitting four chairs and we
used the chairs for lounging around when we were
not in bed sleeping. Since George and I spent most
of the daytime at Granny's house while our mother
was at work, the chairs were put to little use.

We would sometimes eat our evening meal at Granny's house with some of my younger uncles and aunts, who still resided as teens or preteens with Granny, who was their mother. After the evening meal, we would watch television in a large room adjacent to the kitchen, which served as an informal dining area and recreation room.

The televisions showed images only in black and white. There were no color televisions back then. There was only one television channel for viewing and it was WECT Channel Six. Westerns and war movies that depicted events of World War II were our favorites. I noticed that only a few Black People played roles in the television features. Black People were referred to as Negroes and were either house servants or people who did other menial labor jobs in the televised features or skits. They were depicted as servant to the White People, who played various roles on television.

I am pointing out the differences in televised roles because this was a measuring rod for, where we were at in regards to racial equality during the past, when compared to where we are at now. In actuality, only a small percentage of the predominant race of people in this country (Whites) during that era, were engaged in radical behavior, which was uncomfortable to most people. However, those people, who had radical beliefs in the superiority of Whites, ensured the rules that limited the interactions and associations between Whites ands Blacks were followed. To prevent conflicts with the radicals, some Whites either condoned their behavior or ignored the radicals.

There were often constant reminders. I would hear on the radio during the nineteen fifties and nineteen- sixties that a Negro man or several Negro men had been arrested at specified locations for robberies or other crimes. Blacks were referred to as Negroes during those times. This was one of the rules that were used to distinguish, which person by race had committed crimes. Under the rules, if the persons who had committed the crimes were white, then no mention would be made of their race. In this way, people could determine what race of person had committed certain crimes. However, it was intended that the whole population of the City of Wilmington, North Carolina, would know when a Negro or Black had committed a crime.

Nowadays, no mention is made of the race of the person who committed certain crimes, but the name of the housing project, subdivision or village is used. Since specific races of people populate some areas of cities heavily, the mentioning of specific areas seems to serve the same purpose as during the past.

As a five-year old, I dreaded hearing that someone Black had committed a crime. I never dwelled mentally on information about White people that had committed crimes, when it was announced over the radio and television. It appeared to me that only Blacks were bad people, because I was misguided by the way that news was presented about Blacks on the radio.

I did not intend for this story to be a discussion about social issues in regards to the races during the past. However, it is necessary to document such events, because they depict how a race of people was exposed to elements that were intended to lower their self-esteem as humans.

I am going to tell my story, which includes living as a Black in the South during the nineteen fifties and sixties, which was about one hundred years after the Emancipation Proclamation. But at the same time, I am going to expose beliefs of the supernatural and witchcraft, which played a significant role in the past and even now in the present time, in keeping the Black race contained.

I must point out that my ancestors brought conjuring or witchcraft to this country from West Africa. I have read excerpts compiled by white missionaries who ran religious missions in West Africa.

The missionaries documented that conjuring or witchcraft was sometimes an evil affair and used to destroy people's lives by either its use or implications. Some of the excerpts that I read concerning the use of certain talismans or spells, are relative to the folklore I have overheard from older Blacks here in America.

Even today, the folklore and beliefs about conjuring or witchcraft still exists in the rural south. Because Blacks migrated from the south and settled through out this land, the beliefs about conjuring are mentioned everywhere. I found it incredible that most Whites, whom I often have conversations with, have no knowledge of conjuring when compared to most Blacks.

Though the missionaries documented information in books about witchcraft practices, from several hundred years ago, it is relative to practices I have heard described by Blacks during modern times.

Though Blacks and some other cultures use magical incantations, spells, and talismans as reprisals or revenge against others, people of other societies, use physical attacks instead to achieve the same goals or objectives. It appears that the supposed use of witchcraft or conjuring prevents the shedding of blood to some degree. However, the practice of conjuring destroyed some people mentally instead of physically. It is difficult to compare the effectiveness of conjuring versus physical attacks against others.

There are also Whites in this country who are involved with witchcraft and this can be traced back to Europe where their ancestors originated. European witchcraft still has influence in the lives of some Whites. In fact, a White man, who was German born, immigrated to this country during the 1800s, and researched Blacks involvement with conjuring in this country. He also studied the Native Indian witch doctor and medicine men methods and wrote a book which incorporated European witchcraft, African American conjuring and Native Indian magic. I learned that this book is often use by many practitioners of witchcraft in this country. The book was written during the 1800s. I will not ivulge its title, because I do not encourage the practice of witchcraft. I hope that the strange and tragic events portrayed in my novels will encourage others to refrain from this also.

We would live in our shanty for about a year and then my father, William, would reunite with my mother. We would then move to the city of Wilmington with him. Since my father was still carrying a heavy burden because of the killing of his mother, we as a family would suffer physically and mentally from the abuses and neglect of my father.

The tragic intervention by my maternal grandfather did little to correct the negative lifestyle of my father, William. Under the circumstances, the tragedy of 1957 should have changed my father's ways, after the loss of his mother. However, my father was never able to grasp the significance of the tragedy and did not use it to change himself in a positive way.

These situations will be discussed and outlined in the second sequel to this book. However, I have now come to the end of this book's chapter about members of my family and their strange and mysterious lives.

Nowadays, I remember looking out the windows of our small shanty, as a five year old, at the woods and trails that snaked through the woods. I use to daydream about trekking through the woods on an adventure. But now these thoughts are just mere memories of the past, when life was so simple and carefree. One day I will walk to where our shanty once stood and reflect on the kind days of my youth, while living near my maternal grandparent's farm. This was the best time of my life, because our move to the city during the year nineteen sixty-one to reunite with my father would be the beginning of turmoil, revenge and anguish.

CHAPTER EIGHT

The Day of the Mule

I remember awakening one morning and after getting dressed, I went to Granny's house to spend the day while my mother was at work. I noticed that Granny was upset that winter morning of 1960, because her mule was discovered dead during the early morning hours. There was suspicion that a man, who had asked Uncle John for some spare oats had killed the mule. Uncle John had refused to give the man some oats and an argument ensued between the men. My relatives suspected that the man poisoned the mule.

Granny was very upset and exclaimed, "There some terrible people living on this earth. To kill a poor mule for no reason at all. What is this world coming to?" I noticed over the course of the years that Granny would always say, "What is this world coming to" at the end of conversations that described bad things that people had done. It was always her closing sentence during such conversations.

Though Granny was venting her frustration over the mule's death, she was continuously preparing the morning meal. Without doubt, Uncle John and Uncle Leon would need a heavy meal to sustain them during the digging of a huge pit to bury the mule in. Uncle Leon stayed home from school to help Uncle John dig the pit. They also drove Uncle

John's Studebaker car to the hardware store and bought several hundred pounds of quick lime. The lime would be thrown in the pit over the horse to accelerate its decay and reduce odor.

I looked at the mule, which was sprawled out on its side. It was a cold winter's day during February of 1960, therefore the cold made their task somewhat easier. There were no insects buzzing around the horse due to the cold weather. Despite the mule being positioned on its side, it still looked huge.

Uncle Leon and Uncle John took some shovels from a storage shed and began digging the pit. I stood at a considerable distance away from them while they dug. Within an hour, both men were knee deep inside of the pit. An hour later they could only be viewed from the waist up, as the pit got deeper. Three hours after they begun their task, both of my uncles could no longer be seen, except for their upper arms, which was throwing shovels, filled with dirt out of the pit. Another hour went by.

Finally, Uncle John and Uncle Leon emerged from the deep pit and attached ropes and chains to the mule's legs. They attached the lengths of ropes and chains to the rear of Uncle John's car. Uncle John then drove his car towards the pit with the dead mule in tow. He turned the front wheels of his car sharply to avoid the pit. As he drove past the pit, he then corrected his turn and towed the mule over the open pit. The mule fell inside the pit with a thump and my uncles completed the grisly chore by throwing bags of quick lime into the pit on top of the mule's carcass. Uncle Leon and Uncle John then threw spades of dirt into the pit and filled it within a short time.

A few days later, another mule, which was big like the one that my uncles buried, was brought to the farm in a horse trailer. The trailer was towed by a pickup truck. A mule was critical to our farming operation and Granny, who was renowned for her thriftiness, had cash money for its purchase. During the nineteen fifties, people residing in the rural areas or country were very thrifty and resourceful. Money was only spent for the bare necessities or essentials. There was no waste of money or materials on a farm. Uncle Leon would use discarded pieces of lumber and build rabbit box traps. We had wood burning stoves for heating and cooking. Discarded wood was also used for those purposes.

My family and I are country folk. We plowed, planted, and harvested the land. Though those days are now gone, we can still envision those days of toil. We fed others and ourselves from the bounty harvest of the land.

Now, I stand here proud and strong. I caress the land's beauty with my eyes. I smell the sweet fragrances of honey sucker. The dusty wet smell of rain pelting against the dusty soil assails my nostrils, though it is raining miles away. The rain will be upon me soon. I stand and wait.

Suddenly, from the sky above, the rain cascades down upon me and soaks my body and clothing. Come rain and nourish this land of ours. Stay for a while. We are very thankful. We give praise to our creator for this gift.

EPILOGUE

I hope that you enjoyed this sequel. There will be an additional sequel, which will disclose how refusing to forgive drove one of my relatives to ruthlessness. This true character was corrupted by past events, and consulted with practitioners of the black arts to get revenge. It has been foretold that over time, people related by blood will commit acts of evil against each other.

I encourage others to rid themselves of hate and practice the art of forgiveness. Then we can heal and continue our life journeys in a profitable way.

May your lives be fulfilling and I wish you prosperity.

THE END

ABOUT THE BOOK

The author continues the dramatic and tragic real life story about his family's secret. His previous novel, which critics and readers have given rave reviews, sat the stage for sequels to his dramatic story. Readers demanded sequels to the previous novel. The author agreed to quench their thirst with more true drama about his family.

In this dramatic true story, the author finds and visits for the first time the grave of the relative who perished during the great family tragedy, though it is forty-five years after the tragedy occurred. The event was filmed by the author's hometown television station.

In this offering, the author, Willie Tee, explores in depth the issues and problems that caused his family's burdensome tragedy during nineteen fifty-seven on his maternal grandparents farm. The tragedy would be kept as a secret from Willie, his siblings, and cousins, who were toddlers when the incident occurred. The secret and its burdens were revealed to them when they became teenagers.

A series of tragedies spun from the secret over a forty-year period of time. Perhaps it was coincidental, but this sequel raises some issues that are laden with mystery. This memoir mentions that subsequent deaths and tragedies within the author's family had dates with similar numerical significance. This story explicitly depicts the relativity of dates on which family tragedies occurred. The dates indicate a pattern. It is often said that our lives and its events are destined when we are born. The pattern of dates in which tragedies occurred in the author's family seemed predictable and is eerie.

This story is thought provoking and mysterious. The author has dreams about future events, which mysteriously occur. His presence at events, which may have influenced the outcome, gives credence to this incredible story. Perhaps the author is motivated by destiny to reveal his family's story to readers. Readers will be inspired by this masterpiece of a story.

ABOUT THE AUTHOR

NAME: Willie Tee (pen name)

PERSONAL INFORMATION: Willie was born during 1955 at Burgaw, North Carolina. He attended school, elementary through high school, at Wilmington, North Carolina.

FAMILY: Willie has a wife, Ruth, a daughter April, and a son Frederick, who are adults. Willie resides with his wife and granddaughter, Janina at Chesterfield County, Virginia. Willie has another granddaughter, Lisa Marie, who resides near Bamberg, Germany.

HOBBIES: Willie enjoys travel, fishing, reading, writing essays and poems and chatting on the Internet.

MEMBERSHIPS: Retired U.S. Army Staff Sergeant; The American Legion, Alpha Phi Sigma, Omega Mu Chapter (National Criminal Justice Honor Society); Alumni, Virginia Commonwealth University, Richmond, Virginia; Alumni, John Tyler Community College, Chesterfield Virginia.

EDUCATION: Bachelors of Science Degree, Criminal Justice; Associate Applied Science Degree, Police Science, (Magna Cum Laude).

CURRENT OCCUPATION: Consumer Affairs
Investigator

SYNOPSIS:

Born at Burgaw, North Carolina, Willie Tee
lived in the rural areas at family farms until he was
six years old. Willie's book portrays some scenes of
farm life during the late 1950s. Willie moved to
Wilmington, North Carolina with his parents during
1961 and resided there until he enlisted in the
United States Army Military Police Corps during
1974. He retired from the U.S. Army during 1994
with the rank of Staff Sergeant.

Book Purchasing Information

This book can be purchased through bookstores as a book in print. It can be purchased on the Internet at www.authorsden.com/willietee, www.bn.com, www.booksamillion.com and www.amazon.com.

Purchase the following books or products via mail by sending the purchase price plus $3.00 shipping to: Willie Tee, P.O. Box 5171, Midlothian, Virginia, 23112. Pay by money order or check for the products listed below.

The Keepers of The Secret $11.95.

The Winds of Destiny 2nd Edition, $13.95 for paperback or $24.95 for hardback.

The Winds of Destiny (Audio Book) $18.95.

Please add $3.00 for shipping and handling if purchased via mail.

If you are interested in the 1st Edition of The Winds of Destiny, you can order it at www.authorhouse.com. The 1st Edition is the same as the 2nd Edition but it contains no critic reviews. The 1st Edition is printed on demand in a digital format by computer.